1001

Weird Facts
for Canadian
Gardeners

A.H. JACKSON

Lone Pine Publishing

The Distributor: Lone Pine Publishing

Library and Archives Canada Cataloguing in Publication

Jackson, A. H., 1944-

  1001 weird facts for Canadian gardeners / A.H. Jackson.

ISBN 978-1-55105-616-6

  1. Gardening--Canada--Miscellanea. I. Title. II. Title: One

SB453.3.C2J43 2010   635.0971   C2010-901014-0

Editorial Director: Nancy Foulds
Editorial: Sheila Quinlan, Wendy Pirk
Production Manager: Gene Longson
Design & Layout: Volker Bodegom, Rob Tao
Cover Design: Gerry Dotto
Photos: front cover photo © Richard Georg, istock; back cover photo
          Obedient Plant by Tim Matheson; title page photo © photos.com

PC: *1*

Contents

ACKNOWLEDGEMENTS

John Troyer's father was an herbalist in Switzerland before he immigrated to Pennsylvania around 1750. John was born there in 1753. He married a girl named Sophronia, and they had two children, Michael and Barbara. Then along came the American Revolutionary War, and while he bore no arms for either side, the political situation forced him to pack up and move to Canada in 1788. A good thing, because I owe John Troyer my interest in plants, especially the weird ones. If he had not moved north, he would never have buried the little wooden box on a Long Point beach, and I never would have found it while searching for lost bottles of Prohibition-era whisky.

Hunting for flotsam whisky is a curious summer job for a teenaged boy, but nearby Port Dover had been a major shipping point for Prohibition smugglers. Their *modus operandi* was to run 50-bottle sacks of whisky out to Long Point in fast boats, mark them with a tiny float and dump them over the side for pick up by their American customers. Storms and American customs boats would now and then disrupt a delivery, and 50 bottles would go a-wandering, eventually to the beach. About a third of the bottles we found were still good, and yachtsmen in Erie, Pennsylvania, would pay us $40 each. Not bad pay for the 1960s—but I digress, so back to John Troyer and his little box.

John homesteaded a section of land near Port Rowan in what is now Ontario. He planted orchards of various fruits, a truck garden and a small plot of medicinal herbs.

John was good with herbs, and the locals called him Doctor Toyer, although some preferred "witch doctor." Locals would visit John to be cured of various ailments and to have lost things found. He could do that, he and a local girl, last name Fick, who also claimed psychic powers. They would sit for hours and stare into a large, polished moonstone until the location of the lost item revealed itself, and it must have worked a few times, since they earned a province-wide reputation as consulting psychics. Their most famous consultation was the solving of the supernatural occurrences at the Selkirk settlement of Baldoon on Lake St. Clair.

For a period of three years, an unfortunate settler named John McDonald had been cursed by a series of mysterious disasters: barns demolished, crops withered, windows shattered, mysterious cattle deaths and fires in the night. Desperate, John McDonald made the trip from Baldoon to the cabin of John Troyer for a consultation. There in the lamplight, McDonald related the story of his mysterious misfortunes, and John Troyer, along with the Fick girl, began to stare into the moonstone. They stared for hours, but finally arose and presented McDonald with a cure for his woes. On his return to Baldoon, he must fashion a silver bullet and shoot a strange white goose he would find within his own flock. When done, he should go visit a widow woman, a neighbour.

McDonald did as instructed, and rifle in hand went looking for his flock. Sure enough, just as Dr. Troyer had said, there appeared a pure white goose amongst his greys, and McDonald quickly raised the rifle and fired. Shot through the wing, the white goose flapped away into woods, honking like a banshee. As instructed, McDonald paid a visit to his neighbour, the old widow woman, and found her hunched into a chair on her small porch nursing a broken arm. The discovery so surprised McDonald that he left without saying a word, but he knew the spell had been broken.

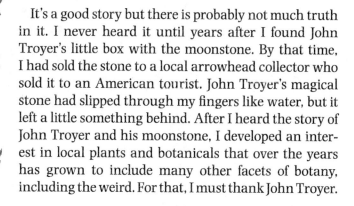

It's a good story but there is probably not much truth in it. I never heard it until years after I found John Troyer's little box with the moonstone. By that time, I had sold the stone to a local arrowhead collector who sold it to an American tourist. John Troyer's magical stone had slipped through my fingers like water, but it left a little something behind. After I heard the story of John Troyer and his moonstone, I developed an interest in local plants and botanicals that over the years has grown to include many other facets of botany, including the weird. For that, I must thank John Troyer.

INTRODUCTION

The dictionary defines weird as involving or suggesting the fantastic or bizarre. It attributes its origin to the early Scots. Weird is derived from *wyrd*—akin to worth, or fate. Think of "double, double toil and trouble," the famous line uttered by the Werde sisters, the three witches in William Shakespeare's play *Macbeth*, while they stirred their poisonous caldron of toads, newts, hemlock and slips of yew. Odious stuff, and while bizarre in Shakespeare's time, the modern Canadian garden is capable of producing a witch's brew that makes the Werde sisters' concoction look like chicken soup. Alkaloids, amines, glycosides, oxalates, phytotoxins, gaseous oxides of nitrates, heavy metals and compounds causing photosensitivity are all being cooked up in your garden by plants you thought benign and beautiful. That old adage, "what you cannot see will not hurt you," is pure folly for gardeners. Digging in the soil and tending plants can be a dangerous pastime, and you had better know friend from foe.

My first experience with the weird and dangerous side of gardening occurred many years ago at my family's summer cottage. Our neighbours, an elderly couple, had decided to clear some brush and construct a rose garden. Their plan was simple enough: chop shrubs, scythe the brush and burn it all. In the old days, people burned stuff; they raked it up into a big pile and threw in a match. I was only eight or nine, and while I did offer to help, our neighbour decided it was man's work and ordered me to watch, learn and keep out of the way. That old boy was in good shape; stripped to the waist

and gleaming with sweat, he worked that scythe like the devil himself. He taught me how to use it on his rest breaks.

Things were progressing famously and I could almost visualize the rose bushes, but then came the striking of the match. Burning green stuff generates a lot of smoke, but our neighbour had a job to do and continued working in the haze. Dragging stuff into the fire, he would disappear from sight, only to emerge seconds later smiling. Man's work indeed, and I remember being mighty impressed; only the next time he entered the smoke he came out screaming like a demon. I was terrified. A real devil had hold of that old boy—and its name was poison ivy. To touch those three poisoned leaves is trouble enough, but to burn them and breathe the smoke is deadly. Our neighbour's clearing never saw a rose bush, and the old boy survived only because an ambulance happened to be in the vicinity when my dad made the call.

My next weird experience with deadly plants occurred some years later at a farm where my dad kept his fatted steers. My dad never did anything by half measures, and that included meat for the barbecue. Dad would buy two calves, have them fattened on grain over the winter and, come barbecue season, he would have a ready supply of thick, juicy steaks. A bit eccentric, but the steaks were to die for—which is precisely what the farmer told my dad over the phone was happening to his twin steers. The steers were dying and the local veterinarian could not figure out why. They were not diseased, and during the night would recover only to have the sickness return the next day. The vet thought poison, but he checked their feedstock and every inch of the pasture and found nothing toxic.

I love mystery and went along with my dad like a young Sherlock Holmes to investigate. Sure enough, the steers were a sorry-looking pair: red eyes, drooling profusely and certainly not the prize specimens my father envisioned for the summer sear. Having only been on that farm once before and in the dead of winter, I took a turn around the pasture fence while my dad palavered with the vet and farmer. It took me a while to return, because I had to explore the bit of swampy forest at the end of the pasture, the section with a new fence. When I did return, I knew the reason the steers were sick. They had been at the new fence eating leaves off nearby trees, and I knew those trees. I told my dad, who told the farmer, who looked at the vet and got a shrug.

Next day the farmer called my dad with news that it was indeed the trees. The vet had confirmed the toxicity of a species that comprised over half his woodlot: poison sumac. All's well that ends well: the farmer cut the trees back from the fence and the steers recovered. They had a good month before winding up on my dad's barbecue. It was a sad end for them, but the farmer was happy and I will always remember what he told my dad, "Smart kid you got there, Mister J." Not so smart, since the year before I had wandered through a patch of poison sumac while hiking with friends and spent weeks slathered in chamomile lotion. The stuff is worse than poison ivy and, once experienced, you will know that tree like your own mother. What's in your backyard?

Gardening is a great adventure, and dangers are slight compared with the rewards. Nothing on earth is as physically and spiritually satisfying as creating your own Eden or providing the family with daily sustenance from a vegetable garden. We come from the earth and depend on it for our very existence; we are God's gardeners charged with nurturing his creations. It's a weird thought, but it comes to every gardener when things are right in the patch: "a little bit of heaven, and in my backyard." Maybe not so weird, as it could be the Creator meant this world to be a class—Heaven 101.

Introduction

God said, Let us make man in our image, after our likeness: and let them have dominion over the fish of the sea, and over the fowl of the air, and over the cattle, and over all the earth, and over every thing that creeps upon the earth.

—Genesis 1:26

Having dominion sounds like mankind is supposed to be a guiding force on this planet and not its major consumer. However, as a Canadian gardener, you are doing your bit and will probably get a free pass to the Creator's redux. Another weird thought, but then this book is all about weird happenings. Weird is such a huge topic, especially when it comes to gardens, places teeming with life both imaginable and unimaginable. There are more individual life forms in your garden than there are people on this planet, and that is far too many. If you want to see weird, as in real aliens, buy a microscope and check out your soil, then turn the scope on some of your favourite foods like applesauce and juice—and be ready for a shock.

Weird garden facts must be started somewhere and since this is my book, I get to choose the where and how. A list of 1001 facts would be boring to the extreme, so I shall create a mélange of factual dialogue, hopefully entertaining stories and, of course, weird facts. We will begin our tour of weird with big, as in those giants of the global garden: wheat, rice and...king corn. And we will finish with tiny, as in nematodes and bacteria.

10

HISTORICAL CORNFUSION

The popular perception that all Canadian First Nations people lived a nomadic hunter-gatherer existence surviving on bush meat, pemmican and found berries is incorrect. In 1535, when French explorer Jacques Cartier sailed to Canada for the second time, he ventured down the St. Lawrence River and discovered an Iroquois settlement called Hochelaga (now Montreal). In his log, Cartier noted the good and large fields of corn. A century later, when La Salle traversed the Great Lakes to the Mississippi, he found huge fields of corn, beans and squash that local tribes depended on for survival. Corn, or maize, was their staple diet and had been for 1000 years.

During the French military campaign against the Iroquois in 1687, the Marquis de Denonville, governor of New France, reported over a million bushels of Iroquois corn destroyed. More than 100 years later, in 1779, when the American Congress sought to punish the Iroquois for siding with the British during the American War of Independence, they sent General John Sullivan and an army of 5000 into Iroquois country with orders to burn and pillage. General Sullivan reported to Congress that the expedition had destroyed 160,000 bushels of corn and cut many thousands of apple trees, 1500 in one orchard alone.

Although a few crab apple varieties are native to Canada, those that General Sullivan found and destroyed were varieties brought from France by early settlers. Micmacs on the east coast had observed

French adventurers planting an orchard at Port Royal in 1606, and when the French abandoned the settlement the following year, the Micmacs waited for the trees to mature and harvested seeds from apples and other fruits. The Micmac were great traders and those seeds became inventory, but the secret of pollination eluded the Micmac, and many years would pass before they could secure beehives for pollination. When that time arrived, both apples and bees entered the native trading network and spread like wildfire across almost the whole of North America.

Aside from vast apple orchards and immense fields of corn, First Nations people cultivated beans, squash, pumpkins, gourds, Jerusalem artichokes and tobacco. Farther south, they grew sweet potatoes and sunflowers. During his mid-17th-century Great Lakes sojourn, the French Jesuit priest Jacques Marquette reported feasting on beans, melons and squash grown by local tribes. He thought the melons and beans first rate but disliked the squash owing to the tribe's habit of drying them in the sun for use in wintertime. In his book, *Histoire du Canada* (1636), the Franciscan priest Gabriel Sagard mentions how the Huron cultivated various crops by tilling the soil with small wooden shovels. The results so impressed Sagard, he wrote, that it was easier to find his way around prairies and forests than Huron cornfields.

Priests aside, the early explorers had sailed to the Americas looking for a way to India and gold. Disappointed at finding neither and not wanting to return to Europe empty handed, they loaded their ships with dried corn, fish and furs. The corn became an instant hit with agronomists in Europe, the furs set a fire under European milliners, and the fish caused mass movement of entire fishing fleets to the New World. Corn was not new to Europe—Christopher Columbus had returned from the Americas with ears of corn in 1492, but his samples had been small, and corn was considered a novelty. From 1492 until Cartier returned, corn seeds were a jealously guarded secret of royal Spanish gardeners and monks. Cartier's cargo changed all that. The seed spread rapidly throughout Europe, creating a huge demand for new corn varieties, of which there were many in the New World. North America soon became busy with opportunists whose only object was to grab as much as they could carry in as short a time as possible. European adventurers sailed to the new land like bandits, robbing, pillaging and killing for whatever they could find. They succeeded, and their cargos changed the diet of Europe.

Adventurers to the New World brought back tomatoes, potatoes, peanuts, pineapples, tobacco, chocolate and a host of new spices. From Canada they brought fish, corn, furs, medicinal herbs and many other treasures either traded or looted from indigenous populations. Native tribes and bands could do nothing to stop the thievery, because arrows and spears were useless against invaders armed with cannon and firearms. The only recourse for native tribes was retreat or connivance, and the Iroquois were good at both. The Iroquois allied with the Dutch, then with the French, until finally trading their lands, furs and corn to the English for the guns they used to steal land, furs and corn from the Huron nation. Arming the tribes became expedient for the warring French and English trading companies; the Hudson's Bay Company armed some members of the northern Cree and Assiniboine tribes to act as protection against their French trading competitors and to act as intermediate traders with more distant tribes. Native peoples were already skilled traders with a network that reached far into the West; flint, copper, deer hides, corn, wild rice and furs had been traded for bison robes, blankets, exotic furs, fresh produce, pottery and dried meat for thousands of years. The Arikara, a Missouri River tribe, operated large trading centres on

the Missouri and Grand rivers with access restricted to tribes of their choosing.

Nobody had to teach First Nations peoples the politics of trade; when European guns and trade goods came along, they knew what to trade, whom to trade with, and what tribes to avoid. The Sioux tribes were not welcome east of the Grand River, in what now is the state of South Dakota, and their existence was kept secret from European traders for years. Just as well, because when it came to being nasty, the Sioux made the cranky Iroquois look like puppies. Trading guns to the Sioux was a no, no, and respected by all tribes in the trading network. However, good politics was soon steamrolled by greed, and when the French, in an effort to stem the tide of English influence, supplied arms to the Sioux, they unleashed a horror on the entire trading system. With guns, the Sioux pillaged the trading centres, decimated whole tribes and collapsed the trading network, forcing European fur traders to trek from their trading posts into the interior.

With no trading network, corn, fresh produce and beaver pelts turned into commodities worth their weight in guns, powder and shot. Among the bad consequences of that combination, trade soon fell into the hands of opportunistic *coureurs de bois.* The stock in trade of these itinerant outlaws consisted of whisky and firearms, a volatile mix that almost put an end to the great cornfields, orchards and gardens of First Nations peoples. "Almost" only counts in the game of horseshoes, because when the French military moved farther south, they found cornfields that stretched to the horizon along with great gardens of produce and orchards all belonging to the Natchez nation. Friendly relations with the Natchez soured when the French seized the corn and produce and ordered tribes to leave specific areas needed to build forts. The Natchez resisted, burned a few French forts, but in the end they were massacred; 500 of the survivors were rounded up and sold as slaves in the West Indies. Quick to learn, other tribes jumped onto this bandwagon, and soon trade with First Nations peoples became a trade in First Nations peoples.

From the gardens and luxuriant cornfields of the New World, the Europeans created a maelstrom of intrigue and violence that ended in total war, with generals like Montcalm and Wolfe leading bands of First Nations warriors on campaigns of vile butchery against settlers and allied tribes. By 1759, General Wolfe had become so inured to human suffering that he ordered his cannon to bombard the unprotected lower town during his attack on Quebec City. There is no proof, but the bullet that killed General Wolfe was English and was probably fired by one his own outraged soldiers.

Pushed westward, most Native peoples tried repeatedly to live in peace and grow their corn, only to be denied a harvest by invaders hungry for land and buffalo robes. During the mid-1800s when civil war raged in the U.S., Native peoples got some respite from persecution, but after hostilities ceased, the U.S. government once again cast covetous eyes on western lands and decided to employ dastardly measures to clear it for settlement. Keeping the enemy sick and hungry had helped the U.S. government defeat the Confederate Army, so why not try it on the Plains Indians. "Kill the buffalo and starve the Plains tribes onto reservations" was the order from Washington, and it worked even better than it had against the Confederates. A new German tanning technology enabled the easier tanning of more hides and a superior finished product. The European market had opened up for buffalo leather, and hunters arriving by railway soon had the Great Plains cleared and the local tribes starving.

Beaten, hungry, their lands gone, the once-great tribes of the New World looked to the rogues their fathers had excluded from the trade network for a last show of defiance, the Lakota Sioux. In 1862, the great Sioux war chief Red Cloud began a military campaign that successfully preserved Sioux lands for eight years until an arranged treaty gave the Sioux title to the Black Hills forever. "Forever" lasted about five years, when an expedition led by Lieutenant Colonel George Armstrong Custer discovered gold in the Sioux's sacred hills. The Sioux ejected the prospectors forcefully, an action that probably did more for Canada than it helped the Sioux, as it caused the U.S. government to look west instead of north. Civil War heroes Generals George Crook and Alfred Terry were at nearby Fort Abraham Lincoln, now Bismarck, North Dakota, with companies of 6th U.S. Infantry and 7th Cavalry supposedly to ensure expansion of the Northern Pacific Railroad into Canada. Crook responded to the Sioux action by ordering them to leave the Black Hills and enter a reservation—an order they refused. Unaccustomed to refusal, Crook mounted up and set off to thrash the Sioux into showing some respect. Upon finding their encampment, General Crook dispatched six companies of cavalry under the command of Colonel "Jumpin'Joe" Reynolds with orders to beat them up real good. Jumpin' Joe found them all right, only they were Cheyenne and they gave as good as they got, causing Joe to vacate the field and leave behind his wounded, an oversight that saw him court-martialled.

General Crook set off the next spring, in the year 1876, with three columns of 1000 troopers and 200 scouts. He got lucky, or maybe unlucky, because his column ran into an equal number of Sioux warriors at a place called Rosebud Creek, where Old Joe took an awful beating. Meanwhile, about 50 kilometres from this action, the war chiefs Crazy Horse and Sitting Bull had camped alongside the Little Bighorn River with 9000 Cheyenne and Sioux warriors all prepared to battle Crooks' entire army to the death. That never happened, because along came the impetuous George Armstrong Custer and his 7th Cavalry. Spotting the encampment and a small Sioux war party, Custer split his forces in a foolhardy effort to cut them off before they could warn the main group. Custer split his troops again, sending half to attack the south while he threw his remaining force at the north end of the enemy encampment. Had he reconnoitred the north end, he would have found the maze of bluffs and ravines that made him late for the party, as his southern force had already come under attack. Vastly outnumbered and under withering rifle fire, Custer's southern force retreated into a wooded area and would have met their end if Custer had not suddenly opened fire from the north, causing most of the attacking Sioux warriors to veer off and head for the new action. What followed was a disaster for Custer and not much glory for either side in spite of the nicely painted battle pictures.

George Armstrong Custer and his 210 troopers died grisly deaths and both the Sioux and Cheyenne never saw their final, glorious battle. However, some good did emerge from that carnage, as Custer's last stand caused such uproar in Washington that any conspiracy to invade Canada was swallowed up in a national rage to avenge the 7th Cavalry. Sitting Bull and his followers high-tailed it to Canada after the battle, to a place near Wood Mountain in what is now Saskatchewan, where all they wanted was to grow corn and live in peace. Only, corn does not grow well on Wood Mountain and the government in Ottawa was not inclined to assist the Sioux. In 1881, tired and hungry, Sitting Bull returned to the U.S. to become an attraction in Buffalo Bill Cody's Wild West Show. He died in 1890 at the hands of U.S. Indian agents. As Sitting Bull lay dying

with a bullet in his brain, his trained horse, a present from Buffalo Bill, raised a hoof to shake hands, or perhaps to salute the departing spirit of a brave man who only wanted to live in peace and grow corn.

FACTS

Druggist John D. Higginbotham's popular 1869 formula for manufacturing whisky to trade with local First Nations tribes is as follows:

Alcohol—1 quart
Chewing tobacco—1 pound
Blackstrap molasses—1 quart
Jamaica ginger—1 bottle
Water q.s. [a quantity sufficient to do the job]

Boil until ripe.

A cup of the above concoction was traded for one tanned buffalo hide.

In 1868, a train belonging to the Kansas Pacific Railroad travelling across the Great Plains of the American West stopped for eight hours while a herd of buffalo crossed the tracks. Fifteen years later, government agents counted only 835 buffalo roaming the Great Plains; a few years later, only 50 remained.

Technically, buffalo (Cape buffalo and water buffalo) inhabit the plains of Africa and parts of Asia. The scruffy beasts found in North America and some parts of Europe are actually bison—in the same family, but a different genus.

Corn Bloat

In his book *The Omnivore's Dilemma*, Michael Pollard blames corn for historical and modern American cultural problems. Overproduction of corn during the 19th century turned Ohio Valley farmers into whisky distillers and flooded America with cheap, tax-free booze that culminated in a national prohibition during the 1920s. With whisky under tight control, corn farmers turned to convincing the American public to consume surpluses through science and clever marketing. Over the years, scientists and marketers became adept at moving cheap calories, and what those American statesmen Thomas Jefferson and John Adams had called "the Alcohol Republic" slowly became the Fat Republic, as corn is now an ingredient in almost every processed food Americans consume. Where America goes Canada follows, and it too suffers national bloat from a deluge of high-fructose corn syrup.

Obesity in Canada is a promotion of clever marketers and sales experts who jumped ship from tobacco to corn. There are no more cigarette lighters in new vehicles—nowadays your new car or truck comes with multiple drink holders to facilitate the "super-sized" corn-sweetened soft drink that comes along with your super-sized, corn-fattened burger and corn oil-fried chips. *Sitting Bull's Revenge*, the movie, is best viewed with a super-sized drink and a giant bucket of popcorn.

Facts

7-Eleven's Double Gulp corn-sweetened, 64 ounce, super-sized soft drink contains approximately 50 teaspoons of sugar and 800 calories.

If a 3 kilogram baby grew at the same rate as a commercially raised, corn-fed turkey, it would weigh 680 kilograms at age 18 months.

Is nothing sacred? In 2008, the Ontario Corn Producers Association issued the following notice to its members: The demand for bland, less-filling beer, especially in the U.S., has permitted use of more refined carbohydrate sources of two types: A) dry adjuncts, primarily dry milled corn grits, broken rice, refined corn starch and, more recently, dextrose, and B) liquid adjuncts, namely corn syrups.

Most Canadian beers contain sugars derived from corn.

Corn, squash and beans—the basic diet of Native Americans—is called the Three Sisters planting by botanists and historians. Strange how those sisters keep popping up in history; the Greek Fates, Shakespeare's Werde sisters and, in the New World, corn, beans and squash all the way from Canada to the very tip of South America. The sisters grew better in some places than others, and superior seeds were traded the length and breath of the Americas. First Nations tribes bartered better seeds for 1000 years before the Europeans entered onto the scene, and they had hybridized many varieties. Europeans found corn in five main varieties: sweet, popping, flint, flour and dent. Mostly they found dent, a cross between flint and flour corn, and the variety found in Canadian fields and gardens today. The next time you cook up some cobs or open a can, look for the dimple in a kernel, the dent.

The Bible mentions corn 102 times, and no, it is not an error, because when the Church of England introduced the King James Version of the Bible in 1611, the word "corn" meant any cereal grain. When maize arrived on English shores, people called it Indian corn (meaning Indian grain), but it soon became such an important English food crop the word "corn" took on a singular meaning.

At the turn of the century, in 1900, Canadian farmers had 300,000 acres of corn under cultivation with a yield of less than 65 bushels per acre. In 2007, farmers had more than 2 million acres under cultivation with a per acre yield of 165 bushels. It's a lot of corn, around 10 million tons, and piled up it would look something like Mt. Everest. What do we do with it all? We feed about half to livestock, export about 15% and use the rest to make more than 100 products: wallboard, paint, synthetic rubber, margarine, starch, biofuel and sweetener. The last two are the driving, mountain-building forces, but so far, biofuel is a financial dog's bone that depends on subsidies, while the sweetener in corn is getting bad press and with good reason.

Milling corn into starch and treating it with the chemical alpha-amylase produces a mix of simple sugars called oligosaccharides. This slurry is treated with glucoamylase, an enzyme produced by the fungus *Aspergillus* that converts the oligosaccharides into glucose, or corn syrup. The corn syrup is treated with another enzyme, xylose isomerase, and refined into a mixture of 55% fructose and 45% glucose, the ubiquitous HFCS,

high-fructose corn syrup. HFCS is in almost everything we eat and drink, and too much can cause medical problems. It can make you fat, it can make you lean, it can take the hair right off your bean. Nasty stuff, as too much can damage your liver, cause diabetes and put on the pounds. In my neighbourhood, Coca Cola produces a Passover version of their famous beverage using cane sugar, and if you can find it, stock up on a few cases. It tastes better and will have you wondering why they bother with the ersatz corn sugar, especially when the science says "no, no, bad stuff." Manufacturers get high-fructose sweeteners from the ubiquitous dent corn and as consumers await its removal from their food and drink they can turn for solace to another variety of corn, one with a built in happiness factor: popcorn.

Popcorn

My gourmet popping corn pops up fluffier and lighter than ordinary popping corn. Eats better, too.

—Orville Redenbacher

Canadians consume over 2 billion litres of popped popcorn annually, and while most consider it just a tasty snack to munch at movies or in front of the television, it does have an interesting history. People have been enjoying the popped happiness for a very long time. Excavations in a central Mexican cavern known as the Bat Cave turned up ears of popcorn that were radio-carbon dated and found to be almost 5600 years old. Ceramic popcorn poppers dating to pre-Incan times are found in excavations on Peru's north coast, some so elaborately decorated as to suggest royal usage.

The exact origin of popcorn is a mystery, but when Christopher Columbus set foot on the island of San

Salvador in 1492, the Carib Indians tried to sell his crew popcorn. A few years later, when Spanish conquistador Hernan Cortez encountered the Aztecs in 1519, their nobles were decked out in garlands of popped corn they called *momochitel*, a revered foodstuff thought to be a treat from their gods.

At the first so-called Thanksgiving feast at Plymouth, Massachusetts, members of the Wampanoag band of indigenous peoples brought sacks of popcorn as gifts. The little treat drew favour from colonial wives, who soon had it on the breakfast table mixed with milk and sugar, the first breakfast cereal. Those wives had many varieties to choose from, as popcorn came in every colour and size imaginable, but all yielded the same belly-filling amount of fluffy, popped kernels.

In later years, popcorn became the snack food that helped build a nation, literally, because in economic hard times, it became the comfort food almost everyone could afford. During the bleak Depression days of the late 1920s and early 30s, a large nickel bag of popcorn was available on almost every street corner, popped hot and fresh from a machine invented in 1885 by Chicago, Illinois, candy maker Charles Cretors. Cretors' machine produced wonderful tasting popcorn, and demand soared. Soon the machines were everywhere that people gathered: sports stadiums, railway stations and, during the roaring part of the 20s, outside every movie theatre. Popcorn became so popular with moviegoers that Cretors' machines soon moved into the theatres to become the nucleus of the ubiquitous refreshment stand. The very same machine is still there today, tantalizing moviegoers with aromas and tastes synonymous with a night at the movies.

The secret to movie house popcorn is simple: heat the kernels in artery-clogging coconut oil while stirring continuously. When popped, slather with more coconut

23

oil and lots of salt. A medium-sized box of movie popcorn will supply your dietary fat and salt requirements for the next three days, but if you air pop the stuff and leave off the topping, popcorn does indeed make a nice light snack.

Back to the Squash and Bean Sisters

Corn is a hungry crop and needs a constant supply of food: nitrogen. Initially, First Nations growers included a fish head when planting corn seeds, but that practice became redundant when corn's two sisters arrived in the trade network: runner beans and squash. Runner beans fix nitrogen into the soil, a lucky pairing probably stumbled upon accidentally and used to sweeten trade in better seeds. "Psst...buy my two-seed pack and get a really big crop. Plant this one to grow the corn and when the stalk is waist high, plant the other seeds next to it and allow the vine to crawl up the cornstalk. My seed packs are expensive, friend. They will cost you all your hides, and if you had any more, I could sell you another secret seed. One that will save your back from having to remove weeds."

Hide hunters who bought seeds probably suffered verbal abuse from wives until the crop ripened, then it was hurry back to get the other secret, the squash seeds. Squash has broad leaves that inhibit weeds, deflect sunshine and conserve moisture in the soil. Corn, runner beans and squash, the Three Sisters of the New World and a fortuitous agricultural triumvirate worthy of a 3 by 3 metre spot in your garden.

Growing a Three Sisters Garden

You will need a full-sun 3 by 3 metre area. Work the soil well, mix in plenty of compost or aged manure (bean nitrogen won't be available to the crop until next year) and form 15 slight mounds with flat tops. In every other mound, deposit four corn seeds in a square configuration. When the corn stalks are waist high, weed the area and plant four scarlet runner bean seeds four fingers distance from each corn stalk. In your vacant mounds, plant four seeds of your squash or pumpkins. When the bean and squash seedlings emerge, thin to only two plants per mound—easy, neat, low maintenance and a cornucopia of ancient treats for discerning gardeners. If you want to put a harvest smile on the faces of friends or family, include a mound of happiness, a few seeds of popcorn.

FACTS

Corn has been cultivated in Canada for over 800 years. Aside from wild rice, all other Canadian grain crops are of European origin.

Corn is a commercial crop on every continent except Antarctica. On the North American continent, over 93 million acres are devoted to the raising of corn.

Corn is so efficient at photosynthesis that Canada's annual crop of over 2 million hectares produces enough oxygen to meet the respiratory requirements of the entire nation.

The province of Ontario grows 98% of Canadian corn.

One bushel of corn will sweeten 400 cans of soda pop.

FOOLING
MOTHER NATURE

Our planet is overpopulated, over-urbanized and careless with toxic wastes. Mankind is making a cesspool out of paradise and failing the Creator's steps to heaven test big time. Overpopulation is a global political hot potato, and a failure to address it will eventually lead to disaster. Climate change, melting polar ice caps, depleting ozone shield, increasing carbon dioxide in the atmosphere and disappearing soil are all symptoms of a global disease called...overpopulation.

The United Nations predicts that by the year 2050, the world's population will be almost 10 billion, and if steps are not taken to reverse this abominable increase, nature will do it for us in a most unpleasant manner. It will begin in impoverished countries with overcrowded cities; an epidemic of disease will cut off food distribution, forcing hungry survivors into an unreceptive countryside. Rural towns will close ranks and become fortresses against predation by foraging mobs of armed city folk desperate for food. Developed countries will send aid—but historically, emergency aid never reaches the needy and will only fuel terrorism. Terrorism will become rampant and close many borders and international shipping routes. Oil will become scarce in developed nations, imported foods a rarity and global paranoia will rule.

Not a pretty picture, but in the end the world will have adjusted the birth rate and imparted a brutal lesson. What can the developed nations do to help rein in global populations? They can stop forgiving the debts of borrower nations, stop gifting money and make aid to needy countries conditional on lowering birth rates and controlling the depletion of forests and agricultural lands. Hunger is already a huge problem in poor and developing countries, and politicians are once again thinking to fix it by implementing another green revolution spearheaded by biotechnology companies like Monsanto, Dupont, AgrEvo and Novartis.

Readers who remember the first green revolution from the 1950s to 1970s are probably acutely aware of the global economic conditions that existed in those years: it was a time of cheap everything and newly discovered high-yield crop varieties. Cheap oil and fertilizer saw those high-yield crop varieties planted and harvested around the globe; it was a boon for civilization and national populations responded accordingly. When the era of cheap ended, farmers could no longer afford their new crops' ravenous appetite for fertilizer, and those in have-not countries abandoned new for old with yields inadequate to feed their increased populations. But hard times spawn inventiveness and, sensing financial opportunity, the huge biotechnology companies are once again touting green revolution, this time with genetically engineered crop varieties that make the first green revolution's crop yields look like pennies to dollars—their dollars, because the seeds are sterile and if farmers want 'em they gotta buy from them.

Can you see the weird problem? Global agriculture is taken out of the hands of farmers and put into the control of a small number of large conglomerates, some of which already own a good percentage of international food distribution. Farmers farm—that is what they do best—and turning them into serfs for the bioconglomerates is a recipe for disaster.

Bad enough, but other genetically altered seed products from the biocompanies are not sterile and offer

a more insidious threat to traditional farming practices. Plants know procreation means survival and they are very good at it, and while the biotechnology companies claim they can control engineered food crops, it is pure speculation. Pollen flow is impossible to control, and engineered crops will spread their genes to crops in neighbouring fields, thus depriving farmers of choice and creating a legal quagmire. If that neighbouring farmer grows the same crop and saves seed for planting, some of those seeds may contain engineered genes.

Biotechnology companies already have crop police roaming rural areas taking midnight samples from fields near to farmers growing their engineered crop. If they find their gene marker, they use the courts to beat neighbouring farmers into either buying their brand or changing crops. It is a huge problem for farmers in areas dedicated to growing specific crops like soybeans and corn.

Pollen flow from engineered crops will also disqualify farmers from an "organic designation," as the new gene will contaminate the purity of their seed. Can you see the problem here? Big corporate farms are the buyers and planters of engineered crops, while the small farmer, more inclined toward planting organic, will suffer.

It's an old story, big beating on small, but where agriculture is concerned, in the end the consumer also suffers from lack of choice. Engineered crops already stock the produce department of your local supermarket: a dozen varieties of apples, six of lettuce, four tomato, four potatoes, two cucumbers—and you get the picture. Without small farmers, we get assembly-line food that looks great, ships perfect, ripens on time, but is almost tasteless. You can do yourself and society a big favour by frequenting local farmers' markets and buying heritage fruits and vegetables. If you have never eaten a heritage snow, grey or ice apple, you are in for a taste experience.

FACTS

In 1811, immigrant farmer John McIntosh was clearing land on his farm near Dundela, in what is now Ontario, when he happened upon the remnants of an old orchard. One of those old trees bore fruit of a kind John had never seen or tasted. Intrigued, he dug up a few seedlings and replanted them into a clearing behind his house. By 1835, with John selling the ubiquitous McIntosh apple from his orchard, his son Allan began selling the rootstock of his father's unique tree. Today, over 300,000 McIntosh apple trees exist around the world; and every one is related to that wonderful chance discovery of John McIntosh.

An average-sized apple contains more fibre than a bowl of cold cereal, and 80% is soluble fibre, fibre that aids in the reduction of high blood cholesterol levels. Apples are also a good source of vitamin C, supplying about 10% of the daily requirement.

Genetically Engineered Foods

Growing food crops is a risky business: fields are constantly under attack by insects, molds, bacteria and inclement weather. Spraying with deadly chemicals is the normal practice to slow or combat threats from the first three, but pesticides are expensive, can be washed off by rain and have a way of showing up in the ripened product. Weather can finish off a farmer's crop through hail, storms or drought, and it is a common reason for farmers giving up on the land.

These are big problems, with a tiny fix—some plants have figured out how to combat mold, disease and foul weather through adaptation. These plants have figured out how to survive onslaughts and have fixed that

survival technique into their genetic structure. The genes in some plants produce chemicals that are toxic to molds and bacteria, while in others a gene will close down parts of the plant, enabling it to survive a mauling by weather or drought conditions.

It takes no rocket scientist to conclude that borrowing genes from one plant and placing them into another would benefit farmers immeasurably. Sounds like a good idea, and the technique of borrowing is relatively simple; scientists cut the beneficial gene from the host using enzymes and replant it into another cell using a vector, either a bacteria or virus. However, the implanting may create problems; it is a technique akin to doing heart surgery with a shovel. Bioscientists implant these genes on a hit or miss basis, and a miss can be catastrophic depending on the vector used for implanting the new gene. Vectors (the implantation method) can be manual, bacteria or virus, the virus method being most favoured. The problem is that viruses and bacteria have a way of outsmarting scientists by reinventing themselves; the virus or bacteria used to implant the gene can change and threaten the genome structure of an entire plant species. That's bad enough if that species should be corn, wheat or rice, and it's a possible horror story should the vector suddenly transmit from plants to humans.

Beware the new corn, because one bite may be your last. During the 1980s, the U.S. Food and Drug Administration approved a company called Showa Denko KK to use genetically altered bacteria to produce tryptophan, an amino acid food supplement. Well and good, but unfortunately that bacteria developed a little self-protection on the side, a toxin that killed 32 consumers and left 1500 physically incapacitated.

The FDA also approved a genetically altered bovine growth hormone that shows up in 80% of milk sold in the U.S., but is thankfully outlawed in Canada. Genetically altered soybeans cause profound allergic reactions in many consumers; in the United Kingdom these reactions spiked to 50% after genetically altered soybean products hit the market. Here is why.

One day in the early 1970s, some bioscientists at a giant chemical company experienced an epiphany, a thought so profound it would change agricultural practices around the globe. It was simple really: make an herbicide fatal to weeds and find a gene to make a food crop resistant to that herbicide. Do that, and they could rule the world of agriculture. The herbicide is glyphosate, a weak organic acid that inhibits a chemical-synthesizing enzyme in newly emerging plants. Without these essential enzymes, the emerging plants wither and die and, hallelujah, no weeds on our lawns. Spray the stuff after food crops have emerged, and there will be no weeds in the garden, big or small.

However, the scientists at that huge chemical company saved the rest of their epiphany (the genetically altering of food crops to be glyphosate resistant) until the patent ran out. Now farmers could plant and forget about weeds, a truly brilliant concept. However, weeds, the most adaptable of plants, are fighting back by borrowing the altered gene from the glyphosate-resistant crop and turning themselves into super weeds.

Estimates are that 70% of food items stocking the shelves of Canadian supermarkets contain some genetically modified (GM) ingredients. Is it toxic to humans in the long term? Some scientists say yes, others no, but nobody really knows for sure. Studies done by independent labs were found to be compromised by the biochemical companies, and the toxicity question is still left hanging. I suspect one day GM foods will do the world a great harm, but, like other scientific advances, we will have to wait and see what happens and be the

guinea pigs. In the end, weeds may be the sole benefactors of those bioscientists' epiphany.

FACTS

(Courtesy of the Nature Institute)

Atlantic salmon fed *Bt* corn developed altered enzyme activity in livers and intestines, and showed marked difference in white blood cell counts.

Peas engineered to be weevil resistant elicited immune reactions in mice.

Insulin-storing potatoes had higher alkaloid content, and pigs that fed on them had reduced daily weight gain.

A diet containing glyphosate-resistant soybeans affected the nuclei of liver cells in mice.

Transgenic DNA from glyphosate-resistant soybeans has been detected in the internal flora of humans.

Fight Back—Plant a Heritage Garden

Neglect has diminished our agricultural gene pool to such an extent that 75% of Canada's traditional crop varieties are extinct, and many survivors are hanging on by slender threads. You can help these agricultural waifs and do yourself a huge taste favour by planting heritage seeds.

Where do you get them? You can get them from dozens of suppliers across Canada that are supported by the non-profit organization called Seeds of Diversity Canada—a group of concerned citizens dedicated to preserving horticultural treasures for future generations of Canadians. Go to Seeds of Diversity Canada's website for a list of heritage seed suppliers. SDC also runs a members' seed exchange and a bookstore with volumes that will open your eyes to what you are missing.

SDC is running the Canadian Tomato Project, and you might want to get involved. SDC has identified over 150 varieties of tomatoes bred or adapted for growing in Canada. They are asking volunteers to grow varieties over a number of years and document the results, and they will supply free seeds to members.

Mmmm, it's a tasty project that may convince you to plant other historical treats, like garlic, of which there are over 100 varieties suitable for growing in Canada—but that is the subject of another SDC study. Membership is only $30 annually, and the benefits to both you and future generations of Canadians are priceless.

Get involved and grow something from our past before it vanishes from our future. Weird is that these varieties are slipping away, while inexcusable is not doing anything to rectify the situation. Canadian heritage vegetables, fruits and even Carolinian tree seeds are available online.

FACTS

The estimated value of British Columbia's 2010 marijuana crop: $7 billion.

Allium ascalonicum is a shallot grown around the German city of Stuttgart. Originally from Syria and prized for its mild flavour, it has become extinct in its native country. Since it can only propagate by manual separation of the bulbs, it is now an orphan species completely dependent on mankind for survival.

Heritage Plants

In 18th-century Canada, if you wanted to eat you had to grow it, and settlers planted with an eye to surplus because extra meant something to trade. Onions and salad greens were most important, followed by potatoes in English gardens and peas in French. Both gardens would also contain pumpkins, melons, beans, carrots, beets, radishes, horseradish, turnips, herbs and wild chicory as a coffee substitute. Some of these garden crops did well and others failed, depending on where the seeds originated. Crops that did well had their seeds saved and became trade items—acclimatized crops that over the years would become as Canadian as pea soup.

Alas, most of those heavy hitter crops have been replaced by hybridized plants that are more disease resistant, faster growing and easier to ship, never mind that they have no taste. Gardeners looking for adventure are urged to explore the huge diversity of heritage Canadian foods for both their taste and the thrill of making old new again. The list of heirloom or heritage plants is long and diverse and is available online from a number of companies. Below are just a few examples.

- BROOMCORN

  Not native to Canada, but once so widely cultivated it has become acclimatized, broomcorn is considered a heritage or heirloom plant. It is an open-pollinator, which means it can reproduce from seed. It is not a real corn, but a low-grade sugar cane introduced into North America early in the 18th century. Cultivation of the plant spread rapidly through North America because everybody needed a good, cheap broom.

By 1850, and acclimatized to Canadian growing conditions through hybridization, the cane grew everywhere, and broom manufacturing ran full tilt in every major city and town. Nothing beats a corn broom for sweeping wood floors, and while still widely used, the brooms now come from Mexico or China. Gone, but not completely down for the count, broomcorn is still grown in tiny patches around the country, most notably at Black Creek Village, a recreated pioneer village on the outskirts of Toronto, where corn brooms are actually made from scratch and sold to the public.

- POTATOES
There are hundreds of potato varieties, and many hybridized in Canada have become heritage or heirloom. Some of these potatoes are multi-coloured, and others come in every shape and size imaginable. Of the 100 or so old cultivars, like Congo, MacIntosh Black and All Blue, most are being saved from extinction by home gardeners. Canadians owe a lot to home gardeners, who keep what was good for the people alive and out of the hands of government bureaucrats bent on the destruction of all but a few disease-resistant, easily grown food crops.

- JERUSALEM ARTICHOKE
This true heritage plant was grown and enjoyed by Native peoples and early settlers alike. A member of the sunflower family, this tuberous plant is being widely cultivated to manufacture fructose and ethanol fuel, so is in no danger of extinction.

What has become nearly extinct is the consumption of the tuber, a real shame, because cooked properly it is scrumptious, with a taste similar to—yes, you guessed it—artichokes.

While similar in look to potatoes, tubers of the Jerusalem artichoke contain a type of starch called inulin that breaks down and becomes mushy when boiled, so steaming is the recommended cooking procedure. After steaming, a dab of butter, a little seasoning and you have a vegetable side or soup ingredient fit for a king.

Jerusalem artichokes are easy to grow and bug resistant, but need rotation as the quality of their tuber will suffer if planted in the same ground year after year.

• APPLES
So many varieties, and so few find their way to consumers. If you are planting a heritage apple tree, scope out what is already growing in your neighbourhood or on the outskirts of town. No point in having a tree that can't be pollinated, but with any luck you will find remnant trees from old, forgotten orchards and be in business. If your luck holds, it will be a 'Snow,' 'Aimson Beauty,' 'Ribston Pippin,' 'Sauvignac' or 'Wealthy.' On the other hand, the tiny honeybees that pollinate your tree may bring pollen from a strange cross and your tree will have apples like no other and make you famous for your wonderful apple pies. Life is an adventure, and gardening doubles the fun.

• MELONS
'Cream of Saskatchewan' and 'Montreal' melons are mouth-watering heritage melons with green or snow-white flesh. All colours except pink and red went out of fashion in the early 20th century, and consumers lost out big time. If you live near

an Amish settlement, keep an eye on their stalls at local farmers' markets because they still grow heritage or heirloom melons. Finding one is a luscious treat, and you get to keep the seeds.

I could go on and on about heritage or heirloom fruits and vegetables; the selection is long and varied and needs study if you want to include one or a few plants in your garden. A visit to a local heritage garden may help in your selection process, but if that is not possible, go online. There are many heritage garden sites run by nice people who are ready and able to help in your selection.

Fooling the Consumer

During the late 50s, almost every kid owned a BB gun. I got mine when I was 10 with the proviso that I keep and use it on a friend's dairy farm. My friend and I shot rats, and while other kids were starting paper routes, we prowled area barns collecting a nickel for every kill. Barns are hot, dry places in summer, and our return to my friend's farm always included a refreshment stop at the milking parlour. Over the years, those rats have become a dim recollection, but those milk parlour stops are indelibly fixed.

My friend's dad milked Jersey cows that produce a premium product, milk with higher butterfat content than the ubiquitous but more productive Holstein, and we know from watching Food TV that taste is in the fat. Chill that unpasteurized, tasty goodness to $-2°$ C and move it around with paddles to keep it from freezing, and you have a beverage like no other.

Weird how most people have never tasted unprocessed milk. Weirder yet is why we put up with having no choices. Consumers take what the dairies provide and like it, never having sampled the real thing.

37

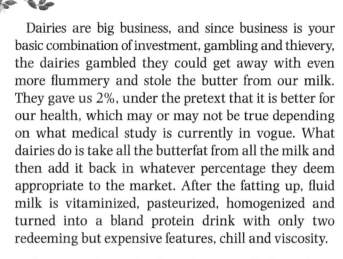

Dairies are big business, and since business is your basic combination of investment, gambling and thievery, the dairies gambled they could get away with even more flummery and stole the butter from our milk. They gave us 2%, under the pretext that it is better for our health, which may or may not be true depending on what medical study is currently in vogue. What dairies do is take all the butterfat from all the milk and then add it back in whatever percentage they deem appropriate to the market. After the fatting up, fluid milk is vitaminized, pasteurized, homogenized and turned into a bland protein drink with only two redeeming but expensive features, chill and viscosity.

If you are thirsty, nothing beats a tall glass of ice-cold milk, and that is simply because of viscosity and chill holding down the quench button on your tongue and throat. It's a sad situation, because every consumer should know they are missing taste, and to have the wool pulled over the eyes of an entire nation is at the very least a criminal act. Older readers may remember when skim milk meant an almost tasteless fluid with a bluish tinge. Not any more; nowadays skim milk is almost indistinguishable from 2%, and for a clue why, check the ingredients list on the carton, the vitamin A palmitate.

Why must dairies add artificial vitamins to a product that is nearly a perfect food? They do it because many vitamins, like the all-important A and D, are fat-soluble and are scooped up with the milk fat, fat that helps the body digest proteins and lay down calcium onto growing bones. The big conglomerate dairies make a lot of money stealing vitamins and butter from the mouths of babes, and the idea of having to return any of it must cause their executives sleepless nights. But what if they found a product where they could keep most of it and substitute cheap vegetable oil and thickeners, like maybe ice cream, sour cream and cottage cheese?

Be on guard, check that ingredient list and make sure the ice cream you buy is actually the real thing and not a frozen dessert made from vegetable oils.

Big food conglomerates love medical studies and are always on the lookout for those they can bend to suit their purposes. All through the 1960s and 70s saturated fats were getting bad press as causes of heart problems. Sensing opportunity, executives of companies marketing vegetable oil conspired with the American Soybean Association to ruin the tropical oil business. Their media campaign was relentless, and in 1985 the ASA sent out a Fat Fighter Kit to its nearly half a million growers urging them to write government officials and food companies protesting the importation of dangerous tropical oils. It worked, and to replace saturated tropical oils, the vegetable oil industry was ready with hydrogenated vegetable oil, and well, you know how that worked out.

I know the food business for what it used to be; I grew up in a food processing family and witnessed the demise of family-run food companies, those small processing concerns where a member of the family was there to oversee every step from field to finished product. Once, while visiting food factories in Europe, my dad had occasion to visit the German food processor Doctor Oetker. Curious as to why no ingredients were listed on any labels, my dad questioned the present-day Doctor Oetker, the son of the founder, and was told, "There is no need for a list of ingredients. My name is on the label."

That is how it used to be in Canada, before the multinational bottom liners bought up everything and NAFTA and GATT rules made it nearly impossible to establish the origin of your food products. Orange juice you think comes from Florida actually comes from Brazil, peanuts in your American-branded peanut butter come from Africa, the fruit in your jam comes from

almost anywhere, brown sugar is white sugar with added molasses, and the sweetness in your soft drinks comes not from cane, but corn. The Canadian consumer is no longer boss in the marketplace and must buy whatever the multinational conglomerates deem appropriate for the shelves.

I saw the end of quality food production in 1976, during a sales visit to a family-run jam company recently bought out by a big multinational concern. I sold that business frozen fruit to make their jams and was anxious to continue the relationship, but all that ended with a big noise. I learned from one of the family members that the new company would be manufacturing pectin jams and jellies, products containing little fruit but lots of sugar. The big noise came from the back of the plant, from the little machine that turned pine 2 × 4s into seeds for their new style raspberry jam.

After 1976, the food business in Canada became the realm of foreign companies depending on chemical additives to compete for limited space on supermarket shelves. Acidifiers, anticaking, antifoaming and bulking agents, emulsifiers, stabilizers, preservatives, colour and the one that makes me laugh, flavour. Unlike food companies of old, foreign conglomerates do not have the Canadian consumers' best interests at heart; they are bottom liners only interested in keeping their investors happy.

Do yourself and your family a big health favour and get off the name-brand lunchtime treadmill. That brand-name peanut butter you feed the kids is half lard; the jam is nothing but colour and pectin; the honey is cut with fructose; the processed cheese is artificial flavour with thickeners; and the soup is so laden with salt you can stand a spoon in it.

The attitude of conglomerate food corporations toward the consumer is best demonstrated by their use of artificial colour and flavour in foods consumed by youngsters. If any food product needs artificial colour and flavour it is probably nutritionally worthless, and marketing such fare to small fry should be a criminal act. Parents should know better—children depend on them to know what is nutritionally good and bad. Frozen French fries contain a chemical formed during the cooking process called acrylamide, a chemical that causes cancer in rats. How is it, then, that big companies can market frozen fries to children?

There are reams of scientific data supporting claims that artificial colours are detrimental to health, but almost every food a child consumes is artificially coloured, and some of those colours are derived from coal tars. During the 1970s, the world's largest jelly-powder manufacturer switched from natural citrus to artificial flavours, and nobody raised an eyebrow, probably because it was the only jelly powder available on supermarket shelves.

One of the big diary conglomerates has become famous in bottom line circles for pulling a monumental fast one on consumers that went unnoticed for years. That company manufactured and marketed many brands of ice cream, but one brand in particular carried a name and graphics that fairly shouted ice cream. With such a strong label connotation to ice cream, the brand could probably sell pudding and consumers would not know the difference. Which is what the scoundrels did, they dropped the dairy, substituted cheap vegetable oil, and put the words "frozen dessert" on the carton. Consumers remained clueless because ice cream is a frozen desert, but obviously not to the pointy headed bureaucrats who aided and abetted this foreign-owned conglomerate in deluding the Canadian consumer.

Many food processors do an admirable job bringing farm production to the tables of Canadian consumers, but there are just as many who consider consumers dupes and suckers to be ripped off through tricky marketing and insider deals with supermarket buyers. Read all processed food labels carefully, especially the ingredient lists. Some of what you find will surprise and shock you. "Hey, there is no cheese in my processed cheese slices!" However, even foods you thought were not processed may provide a shock. "Hey, I thought 'half and half' meant milk and cream!"

If you must buy processed foods, avoid the ones made with trans and saturated fats, and high sodium and sugar. It is much healthier to eat fresh foods, and they taste a whole lot better, so, if you do not already have a vegetable garden, plant one and maybe have a look at canning and jam making. Treat yourself and your family to some quality foods that not only taste wonderful but also are good for you.

Home canning is back in vogue, and no one is better situated to take advantage of this adventurous and rewarding endeavour than the home gardener. Jams, jellies, pickles, relishes, carrots, beans, peas and asparagus spears can all be put up to await your return from the winter vacation the money you saved will provide. You will save, but more important will be the look on your family or friend's faces as they dig into fare the way it used to be, before the bottom line conglomerates stole all the goodness and flavour.

FACTS

In Canada and the U.S., home canning or bottling is done mostly in Mason jars with brass lids, while in the U.K., the container of choice is called a Kilner jar and comes with a glass lid.

Only foods with a high acid content may be canned by boiling, while all others need sterilizing with a pressure cooker.

Clarence Birdseye, father of the modern frozen-food industry, got the idea for quick freezing foods from Inuit fisherman while working as a field naturalist in Labrador. Clarence perfected a two-belt continuous freezing system, and in 1927, he began to market not only fish, but also fruits and vegetables. In 1929, he sold his patents to the Postum Company, a food-processing concern that eventually became General Foods Corporation, founder of the Birds Eye Frosted Food Company.

HALYCHANKA, THE NATION BUILDER

The success of western agriculture began, as many stories do, a long time ago and in a far-away place. That place was Ukraine, a country of vast prairie lands not unlike those of Manitoba and Saskatchewan. Grasses of many types grew wild on the prairies of Ukraine, but one in particular, *Triticum monococcum*, commonly called einkorn, had been cultivated for generations and was used to make gruel and hard-as-iron bread cakes.

Einkorn, a wild grass with 14 chromosomes, is pretty much the granddaddy of modern wheat varieties. In time, the cultivated einkorn crossed with another cereal grass called emmer to produce a 24-chromosome variety, a fact noticed by the women who harvested the grain heads. Why pick skimpy when fatter heads beckon? However, even those fat, easier-to-winnow grain heads made for a miserable fare that needed boiling before baking into gruel cakes.

Then a miracle of sorts happened. The cultivated einkorn/emmer grass crossed with a wild variety called goat grass to produce a 42-chromosome variety, the goat grass being responsible for the gluten needed to make real bread. From those early times up through the 17th century, bread wheat diversified into many varieties, some widely used and some remaining landrace, or peculiar to a region. By the 18th century there were 14 main varieties, and by the 19th century they were being classified as six main classes: hard red winter, hard red spring, soft red winter, hard white and soft white. Spring wheat, the hard and soft along with a variety of hard called durum, are planted in spring and harvested in late summer, while winter wheat is planted in the fall and harvested around mid-summer. Interesting stuff—but just backgrounder for a weird story that helped found a nation, the weird tale of David Fife and his magic seeds.

David Alexander Fife

Dear Farmer Fife: wherever you dwell in the land of eternal light. Please hear me while I thank you for conquering the blight on the wheat crops of our Canada, that give us the might to feed the poor and hungry, so precious in his sight.

—Rosemary John

Born in Kincardine, Scotland, in 1805, David Fife immigrated to Upper Canada in 1824 with his father, mother and five brothers. In those days, settlers had their pick of free land, and the elder Fife chose a section at a place called Otonabee, near what is now Peterborough, Ontario. His section had good loamy soil and good drainage and looked perfect for growing cereal crops. With his sons' help, he cleared the land, tilled the soil and planted oats, barley and white Siberian wheat. The oats and barley did fine, but the yield from the Siberian wheat was disappointing owing to rust and loose smut disease. Every fall they would try the Siberian, but the results were always the same, a fact David attributed to the area's overly cool and damp spring weather. David got into the habit of picking the heads from rust survivors and planting them into a small experimental garden, but the results were always disappointing.

In the late 1830s, David Fife married a local girl, Jane Beckett, and moved a few miles away to his own section, where he planted only barley and kept the Siberian wheat confined to a new experimental garden. In the

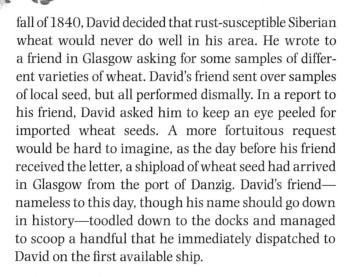

fall of 1840, David decided that rust-susceptible Siberian wheat would never do well in his area. He wrote to a friend in Glasgow asking for some samples of different varieties of wheat. David's friend sent over samples of local seed, but all performed dismally. In a report to his friend, David asked him to keep an eye peeled for imported wheat seeds. A more fortuitous request would be hard to imagine, as the day before his friend received the letter, a shipload of wheat seed had arrived in Glasgow from the port of Danzig. David's friend—nameless to this day, though his name should go down in history—toodled down to the docks and managed to scoop a handful that he immediately dispatched to David on the first available ship.

When David received the packet, he found his friend had scrawled the word "Halychanka" on the outside. At the time, David was unaware of the origin of the seeds or that "Halychanka" meant "Hirka wheat" in Ukrainian. That fall David planted his experimental garden with oats, barley, last year's Siberian wheat and the new Halychanka seeds.

The next spring saw lots of sunshine, few rainy days, and David could not have been happier with his garden. Everything looked perfect—not a sign of rust or loose smut on any of the test crops, and his Halychanka looked robust and ready to mature weeks ahead of the others. Then disaster struck. One morning, when David was in town buying supplies, his wife Jane looked out the kitchen window and saw their cow had broken into her husband's garden. Running outside with a broom, Jane managed to shoo away the cow, but it was too late; the beast had eaten everything. Thinking of her distraught husband, she rummaged about and found three heads of grain from the new seeds David had received from Glasgow, his red-coloured Halychanka.

That fall, David planted his experimental garden with the usual, but without his Halychanka, he lacked expectation. That winter his wife Jane took ill and the small garden took a back seat to getting her well again. By early spring, she had recovered nicely and David could turn his attention to the farm's regular crops and his experimental garden. It was while examining the new growth in the experimental garden that he remembered the three heads of Halychanka his wife had saved and put aside. Thinking it too late for planting, he considered saving them for next season, but decided to gamble. The few seeds of Halychanka went into the ground, with David thinking they probably had no chance.

He realized how wrong he was a few weeks later when his new seeds germinated and rushed to catch up to the Siberian variety. After a few more weeks, they were twice the size and already maturing with no signs of rust or loose smut disease. His Halychanka had crossed with the Siberian white to produce a miraculous new variety. That summer his three Halychanka heads produced a quart jar full of hybridized seed, all of which went into the garden after the spring thaw. Halychanka thrived and with no rust or loose smut they rewarded David with a yield of a half bushel.

Fortune had finally provided David Fife with a break, and being thankful he decided to share with his neighbours, who began calling the miracle grain Red Fife, after the colour and originator. A few seasons later, one neighbour harvested 300 bushels of Red Fife and sold it to the local agricultural society to purify and distribute to area farmers. A few seasons after, Red Fife had so demonstrated its resistance to frost, rust and loose smut that it became the choice crop for the entire Otonabee area. It began to spread across Ontario and into the U.S. Plains states, especially Minnesota, where it fast became the principal crop.

In 1883, William Cornelius Van Horne, general manager of the Canadian Pacific Railway, thought Red Fife wheat was the key to expanding Canada's West. He offered the Winnipeg seed firm of Traill, Maulson and Clark free shipping from Minnesota. The company shipped up to 2000 bushels of carefully cleaned and bagged seed duty-free thanks to the Canadian government. That seed produced a yield of 100,000 bushels, enough to feed the entire country.

In the following years, Red Fife seed traded and sold to new settlers expanded the crop right across the prairies. Van Horne's foresight saw reward in huge shipping contracts to U.S. and Canadian ports, and Canada was well on its way to becoming a world breadbasket. Van Horne's railway whistle stops sprouted grain elevators to store the rivers of red gold, and those elevators spawned towns and cities all the way to the Rocky Mountains.

In 1909, David Fife's stroke of genius and good luck saw replacement by the famous Marquis wheat strain that proved even more frost and disease tolerant than its relative. Marquis is a cross of Red Fife and Hard Red Calcutta—and it is what some prairie farmers still grow today.

Canadian grain farmers and the entire country owe an Otonabee farmer named David Fife more than a plaque by the roadside, and both he and wife Jane should at least have their faces on a note of the realm. Politicians, beavers and birds wind up on our money—why not the nation builders who did so much to make that money possible? David Fife died on January 9, 1877 at age 72, without knowing the impact his beloved Halychanka would have on the entire country. Jane Fife knew—she lived until 1886 and must have died a very proud lady.

FACTS

Per capita consumption of wheat flour in Canada each year is around 44 kilograms.

Canadians each consume almost 14 kilograms of bananas annually—and we share approximately half of that fruit's genes.

Marquis Wheat

Born in London, Ontario, in 1867 and educated at the University of Toronto, Johns Hopkins University in the U.S. and the Sorbonne in France, Charles Edward Saunders wanted a career in music but gravitated to plant genetics for financial reasons. Music paid little, while both his dad and brother Percy had done all right playing with plants. His dad had set up and still ran the Canadian government's agricultural research stations, while brother Percy had helped perfect the Red Fife wheat variety. Charles Saunders gave up his music in 1903 and accepted an appointment as Dominion Cerealist at his dad's station near Ottawa. True, it was nepotism, but fortuitous for Canada, as he had an obsession to improve upon his brother's already improved Red Fife wheat variety.

Unbeknownst to Charles, that improvement had already occurred sometime around 1880 at the experimental station near Agassiz, Manitoba, with a cross between his brother's Red Fife and an Indian variety called Hard Red Calcutta. Problem was, it got mixed with other varieties and grew for years completely unnoticed until 1903, when Charles Saunders visited the Agassiz station. He took seeds back to Ottawa, planted them and subjected the harvest to rigorous testing that included baking his own loaves of bread. In 1907, he sent the harvest back to Agassiz; in 1911, the seed was made commercially available and by the early 1920s Marquis wheat made up over 90% of the Canadian spring wheat crop and 60% of the U.S. crop.

Marquis was a huge success, but it had a problem: it was still susceptible to a disease called rust. By the late 1940s, new varieties of bread wheat had been developed that were not so susceptible to rust, and the mighty Marquis was relegated to the seed archives. During the 1950s, a bioscientist named Norman Borlaug succeeded in hybridizing several rust-resistant wheat varieties and helped usher in the infamous green revolution with its unfortunate effect on global population.

Rust had been beaten off and the world took a breather, but in 1999, out of a tiny wheat field in Uganda, Africa, a new strain of stem rust took to the air and now threatens wheat crops around the globe.

Rust

Cereal crops are subject to predation by bacteria, parasitic nematodes, virus and fungus, the fungi being the most virulent and costly to growers. About 20 fungus diseases attack cereal crops with smut, leaf and stem rust causing the most problems. Smut attacks a plant's reproductive system, producing galls that eventually rupture and release spores onto nearby plants, while rust hijacks the plant's nutrient sugars like a vampire. Rust has been around forever, and while originally a disease of grasses, it has made the transition to cereal crops without missing a beat. The development of resistant cereal crops put rust on the back burner, but it is always around, threatening and nibbling here and there whenever the weather turns wet and warm. Rust has many strains, or races, and each race specializes in a particular cereal plant or plants.

Wheat stem rust attacks wheat and barley; rye stem rust attacks rye and barley; stem rust of oats attacks only that crop; and leaf rusts attack only the leaves of cereal crops. Once a major threat to prairie wheat crops, rust has become a nuisance disease.

All that underwent a change in 1996, when a new race called black stem, or Ug99, arose from a field in Uganda, Africa. It caught a wind to Kenya and the highlands of east Africa, where it decimated wheat crops. In 2007, the black stem rust blew into Yemen and the Sudan, wiping out wheat crops and causing food riots. In 2008, spores were reported infecting fields in Iran, and scientists fear the grain belts of central Europe are next.

It's very bad for them, but what has Ug99 got to do with Canadian gardens? Not much, but if you like a sandwich now and then and would hate to see Canada's wheat fields turned to mush, you will probably want to cheer on the scientists working night and day to put the monster back in its box.

Ug99 has the potential to recreate the Irish potato famine, caused by another fungus, *Phytophthora infestans*, commonly known as late blight. The Irish almost wholly depended on potatoes for sustenance, and the famine of the 1840s decimated a third of that country's population.

Nowadays, about a third of the Canadian and U.S. populations almost wholly depend on corn and wheat. Should another blight strike both countries at the same time, the aftermath is unthinkable. However, we should be thinking long and hard because we have already experienced a few near misses.

During the early 1970s, corn blight stuck at southern U.S. corn-growing states, reducing national production by an alarming 15%. Starting in 2003, a fungus called anthracnose began affecting Canadian corn crops. Should these fungi blow up and begin decimating corn crops at the same time as Ug99 strikes the

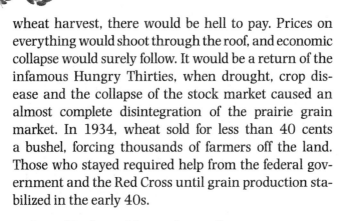

wheat harvest, there would be hell to pay. Prices on everything would shoot through the roof, and economic collapse would surely follow. It would be a return of the infamous Hungry Thirties, when drought, crop disease and the collapse of the stock market caused an almost complete disintegration of the prairie grain market. In 1934, wheat sold for less than 40 cents a bushel, forcing thousands of farmers off the land. Those who stayed required help from the federal government and the Red Cross until grain production stabilized in the early 40s.

That old adage, "do not keep all your eggs in one basket," rings very true when it comes to food crops. Biodiversity is a key to crop survival, and to have countless fields filled with the same genetically modified grains and corn is to invite disaster. However, for the home gardener, those impending threats are more reason to plant heritage seeds and keep on hoeing.

Growing Your Own Wheat

It sounds farfetched, but growing your own wheat can be done in as little as 1100 square feet of space. If you have a lawn that has seen better days and needs replacing, think about giving wheat a try. Your crop of Red Fife will give you a yield of around 30 kilograms of wheat seed that you can then grind in a home food processor. That will provide you enough flour to make about 120 loaves of whole wheat bread—two loaves a week from a beat up lawn you no longer have to mow; not bad. If that sounds too daunting a task, look around for local farmers who seasonally lease small sections of farmland. Grow-your-own is gaining popularity across the country, and some farmers even offer classroom instructions on how to grow and harvest everything from soup sorrel to nuts.

"Hey, Dora! This bread is scrumptious! What bakery did it come from?"

When you explain how you made it from scratch, like the pioneers, your friends will marvel and your esteem will rise like your dough, guaranteed.

FACTS

(Courtesy of the International Development Research Centre)

Wheat is the world's most widely grown cereal grain, occupying 17% of the global cultivation of land. Wheat is the staple food of 35% of the world's population and provides more calories and protein than any other crop.

Asia plants more than half of the developing world's wheat crop. Wheat is also important in eastern and southern Africa, where some countries have seen a 90% increase in consumption during the past two decades.

Rice

Snap, crackle and pop is a huge subject and deserves a chapter, but it is not a product of the grand Canadian garden and will only be touched upon lightly here. Wild rice—the grain that is a product of the grand garden and a member of the grass family like rice and wheat—is a primitive cousin, but is not classified as a true rice. However, wild rice and true rice do have similarities in that both grasses need their roots in standing water, the ubiquitous rice paddy, although true rice needs higher temperatures. China is probably where rice originated, and it seems to have spread from there to other sections of Asia. Nowadays, rice is a global crop, second only to corn, with Asian farmers growing over 85% of the world's production—around 500 million tons in various strains. Rice is the most hybridized food crop on the planet, with thousands of strains, but only few are in commercial production.

Rice is similar to all fruiting grasses in that it has a head of grains atop a stalk, with each grain covered by a husk. Like other grains, husks are removed during harvesting, leaving the brown kernels called paddy, or brown, rice. While some brown rice is packaged and sold, the amounts are infinitesimal compared to white rice, the milled variety with hull, bran and germ layers removed. Many varieties are grown around the world—long, medium and short grain, Arborio, aromatic and waxy—and all have their place in national cuisines. Americans prefer long grain rice and are net exporters of that variety. Long grain contains high amounts of amylose, one of the twin components of starch. Long grain rice does not stick to pots and the grains remain separate after cooking. Medium and short grain rice, popular in Asian countries, contain higher amounts of the other starch component, amylopectin, and the grains have a tendency to stick to pots and each other. Short grain rice is almost round, contains even more amylopectin and is the famous sticky rice.

Many North Americans, especially Canadians, like their long grain rice parboiled, a steaming process that begins when the rice is still brown. Steaming cause nutrients found in the outer hull to move into the grain, making for a surprisingly more nutritious product. The parboiled product is then dried and left as brown rice or milled in the standard manner and put into boxes with a picture of our favourite uncle on the front. I like parboiled rice. I think it tastes better, and while normal long grain has a tendency not to stick to pots but sometimes does, the parboiled never sticks.

FACTS

During the 1970s, a new strain of miracle rice from the U.S. caused Asian rice production to soar, but after a few years, problems arose when the new crop's built-in resistance to disease, called vertical resistance, began to periodically fail. The miracle rice had vertical resistance to a disease called "blast" and an insect pest called "brown plant hoppers." However, when that resistance suddenly failed, both the insects and disease spiralled out of control, decimating the miracle rice and also the neighbouring crops of old, landrace varieties. Widespread famine throughout Asia was the result.

Fried rice syndrome is a disease caused by bacteria endemic to soil called *Bacillus cereus*. In Chapter 5 of this book, "Monsters in the Garden," you will learn about nasty little fellas with tennis rackets called *Clostridium*, which are responsible for some truly horrendous diseases. Although not as vile as *Clostridium*, *B. cereus* uses the same *modus operandi* to make you sick as a dog: spore toxin. Cooking and consuming hot rice will not give spores naturally found in rice the opportunity to release toxins, but problems may arise if rice is allowed to sit at room temperature. To avoid fried rice syndrome, refrigerate rice soon after cooking.

The U.S. grows 12% of the world's rice in six states. Arkansas is the largest producer. The U.S. exports half the crop, while 10% goes into the manufacture of dog food. Woof! Woof!

THE WEED WARS

More energy is expended for the weeding of man's crops than for any other single human task.

—LeRoy Holm, noted weed scientist

The dictionary defines a weed as being a troublesome, valueless plant that grows profusely where it is not wanted. Those few words define a problem so acute that it threatens to upend the world's food supply. For a look at this problem, we must first examine the state of our major domesticated crops, our sources of global sustenance. By domesticated, I mean the plants that have been so altered by man that they no longer exist in the wild, a group that includes almost all our cereal, vegetable and fruit crops. We made them, we need them, we must do battle to keep them. Problem is, outside of the few crops such as corn, wheat and rice, which are so domesticated they depend on mankind for survival, the remainder are ready, willing and able to become feral through pollen flow.

Some weeds are escaped cultivars with a nasty propensity to hang about and threaten crops, while others are simply distant relatives with transgene capabilities to modify commercial crops. A truck farmer has a nice field of radishes and along comes a wind containing pollen from a distant relative. Presto changeo, his cultivated radish crop becomes a field of unmarketable two-headed monsters. The cultivated radish is of the Brassica family, which includes not only a close relative, the wild radish, but mustard as well. The radish outcrosses with a relative, and the progeny can outcross with the cultivated variety. Called novel trait transgene, it is the ability of related species to pawn off peculiarities through gene transference. With radishes, the escaped cultivars (the feral or wild radish) do better with multiple tubers and that novel trait has been set into its genome and pollen. Nice for the wild radish, but a calamity for radish farmers forced to scrap their entire crop. Some vitally important Canadian food and pasture crops have feral relatives—canola, alfalfa, carrot, parsnip, sugar beet and mustard, to name a few—and all have produced feral progeny with many becoming invasive weeds.

GM, or genetically modified crops, have an even greater tendency to wander off and visit relatives, even the dependent domestic crops. In the late 90s, the U.S. government authorized a company called Aventis Crop Sciences to market a *Bt* corn they called StarLink, *Bt* meaning the plant's genome has been altered to include a gene that codes for *Bacillus thuringiensis*, an insecticide toxin. They stipulated the corn be harvested only for animal feed. A year later, the *Bt* gene showed up in corn destined for human consumption, most notably in the tortilla shells of a major fast food chain. In 2000, Aventis withdrew StarLink from the market and the U.S. government began the perpetual testing for *Bt* transgene in corn.

In 1995, Ottawa gave GM canola the green stamp, and while scientists had already predicted the spread of its herbicide-resistant gene, they were surprised at the speed of transgene movement. In just two seasons, government scientists found the herbicide-tolerant gene variant in relative plants across the prairies, some of them invasive. Some scientists fear transgene movements will create herbicide-resistant super weeds as invasive weeds resistant to all herbicides. Super weeds are words that invoke angst in Canadian farmers and

gardeners who fear a confrontation with a super weed terror like kudzu, the infamous vine that ate the South.

I remember a long-ago TV interview with then-President Jimmy Carter, who told the interviewer that in Georgia, he had to move his car every day to free it from the grip of kudzu vines. Canadians should be thankful kudzu is cold intolerant and has no relations in North America. Had it even a distant relative, the mile-a-day monster could be eating up both the American South and North. It has no relatives, but kudzu does have a friend, a copycat vine that is cold tolerant and would love to eat up the north—the Canadian north.

Dog Strangling Vine

Dog strangling vine is a weird moniker for a vine that will not strangle your dog and is actually pale or black swallow-wort (*Cynanchum rossicum*), members of the Asclepiadaceae, or Milkweed, family. Brought from Europe as an ornamental in the mid-1800s, the plant escaped into the wilds of New York State where it began its infamous kudzu-like crawl into neighbouring states and the province of Ontario. Dog strangling vine, or DSV, will cover woodlands, fences, telephone pole, street signs, houses and, if you are not wary, your garden.

Unlike the kudzu vine, DSV is cold tolerant and seemingly indestructible. Once in, this monster will own your backyard, so better imbed its description into your mind and keep close tabs on the dark corners. DSV vine is especially deadly to forests: it will smother tree saplings and prevent germinated seeds from sprouting. This monster loves soil with a limestone base and has found a good home in Ontario and some sections of Quebec. In certain areas of Ontario, the vine can double or triple its normal 1 metre size and completely inundate trees.

Both the pale and black varieties of DSV look and behave the same; the only difference is flower colour.

The black DSV has extremely dark, almost black, flowers and the pale variety's display is pink or red. Flowers ripen to form pods that resemble those of the common milkweed and release their seeds in the same manner.

Eradication of DSV is extremely difficult owing to the extensive root system or rhizomes. Digging it out is all but impossible, because a missed bit of rhizome will spawn multiple heads like a Hydra. Spraying with chemicals is effective but requires multiple applications and is best left to experts. If the beast gets into your garden, mowing it constantly will keep it from going to seed; eventually it may give up the fight.

How did swallow-wort come to be called dog strangling vine? It got that name from the way the tendrils wind about any convenient support, in a circular, strangling motion.

There once was a man from Leeds
Who swallowed a packet of seeds
The silly old ass
Was covered with grass
And you couldn't see his head for the weeds

—Anonymous

Japanese Knotweed

Japanese knotweed (*Fallopia japonica*), not to be confused with other more benign knotweeds found all across the southern parts of Canada, is a big, ugly bully. Once in the door, it will displace other plants to the point of dominance. It is almost impossible to eradicate. A perennial shrub native to eastern Asia and brought to the U.S. as an ornamental during the mid-1800s, the plant escaped into the wild and is now found in most U.S. states and six Canadian provinces. Considered a major invasive weed, Japanese knotweed, *aka* Mexican knotweed, prefers full-sun areas beside streams but will grow anywhere in any soil. It will

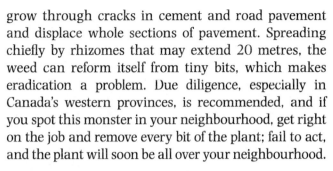

grow through cracks in cement and road pavement and displace whole sections of pavement. Spreading chiefly by rhizomes that may extend 20 metres, the weed can reform itself from tiny bits, which makes eradication a problem. Due diligence, especially in Canada's western provinces, is recommended, and if you spot this monster in your neighbourhood, get right on the job and remove every bit of the plant; fail to act, and the plant will soon be all over your neighbourhood.

The Allergens

• RAGWEED

After the Russians invaded Hungary in 1956, vast sections of arable land became commune-style farms, and poor land management left many once-verdant fields looking like vacant lots. When the Russians left in 1991, the farms sat abandoned while the courts worked out ownership claims. Weeds love abandoned property, especially the weed with a lovely name, *Ambrosia artemisiifolia*, the common ragweed. Nowadays, ragweed is everywhere in Hungary and its infamous pollen has sensitized half the population. Hay fever and asthma are synonymous with *A. artemisiifolia* pollen, and Hungarian doctors are hard pressed to deal with the line-ups that begin in late summer.

A. artemisiifolia is a North American weed species that hitchhiked to Europe on grain and seed shipments during the late 1800s and the Great War. Like most tourists, it took a liking to the European climate and began hanging out in

> *Ambrosia* is from the old Greek language and has two meanings, one the fabled nourishment of the gods and the other the elixir that granted them immortality. English pudding took the first meaning, the king of weeds the second and there never was a name so deserved.

hard-to-find places: behind old buildings, in ditches, gullies and vacant lots, and anywhere the soil had been disturbed. Having no experience with ragweed, Hungarians who did happen to look over backyard fences saw just another weed and not a monster on the attack.

Eradication is almost impossible since a mature ragweed plant may issue a million seeds during a season. Mow it and it grows back in two weeks stronger than ever. Spraying with herbicide may slow it down for the season, but it will be back next year. Pulling it out by the roots is tricky—a touch on bare skin can sensitize and doom the puller to a life of sneezing and snuffling. Ragweed is evil incarnate, and given time will own Europe. Hungary now considers ragweed a threat to national security and has initiated harsh fines for landowners failing to scythe the monster from their property.

In North America, ragweed season runs from July to the end of September, affecting almost 20% of the population and costing billons of dollars in lost productivity and crop damage. Of the 42 global species, 15 are native to North America and three are found across Canada: *A. artemisiifolia*, the common ragweed; *A. coronopifolia*, a perennial ragweed; and *A. trifida*, the giant ragweed. Do the words giant and *trifida* catch your interest? If you have seen that old sci-fi movie *Night of the Trifids*, then you have seen the giant ragweed, because *A. trifida* was the model for those invading horrors. Best have a good look in your backyard—they may be there waiting, just like in the movie.

Giant ragweed can grow to over 4 metres and pump out over a billion grains of pollen every season. Hit them with your weed whacker in season and

61

they will engulf your entire neighbourhood in pollen dust. Actually, from July to September ragweed pollen is omnipresent and covers everything: your skin, clothes, furniture and the family dog. Almost every television news program carries pollen count alerts, and come July they will let you know the day the "king of weeds" lets loose on an unsuspecting public...ahhh, choo!

FACTS

When the first Europeans arrived in Canada, there were no earthworms—none survived the last ice age. The omnipresent Canadian worm found in all gardens is an import that has a weird relationship with weeds. They gather up weed seeds and store them deep in their burrows before birds, mice and insects consume them. Researchers at Ohio State University discovered that earthworms gather up 90% of the weed seeds around their burrow entrances. Why remains a mystery, but it helps invasive weed species.

Weeds cost the Canadian economy around a half billion dollars annually, more than animal disease, plant disease and insect damage combined.

The Contact Poison Weeds

Late at night while you're sleepin' poison ivy comes a' creepin' arou-ou-ou-ou-ound.

—The Coasters

Among the many poison plants in Canadian forests, there exists an evil triumvirate: poison ivy, poison sumac and poison oak. The last is rare, but the others are common as grass yet hardly anyone knows what they look like. "Leaves of three, let it be" are familiar words to nearly all Canadians who know it means poison ivy and better not touch. However, many plants have ternate (three) leaves, and poison ivy grows in many confusing forms. Every summer, Canadian hospital emergency rooms overflow with hikers, canoe trippers, bird watchers, mushroom pickers and casual back-woods strollers all complaining of itchy rash or oozing lesions. The culprit is "urushiol," a plant-produced chemical that binds to the skin, causing an allergic reaction, or what doctors call "contact dermatitis." Nasty stuff, and while around 20% of Canadians are unaffected by urushiol, they too can be sensitized by repeated contact.

A trip to the forest should be a soul-healing experience and should not include an interminable wait for attention in a hospital emergency room. If a trip to the forest is in your future, you had better learn to recognize the herbivores that may do you harm. "Doing harm" is putting it mildly; contact with urushiol causes anaphylactic shock in some people and if not treated can kill.

- POISON OAK
  In Canada, poison oak (*Toxicodendron diversilobum*) is a rarity, and unless you live near either coast, you will probably never encounter this forest nasty. Called oak only because its leaves bear a resemblance to those of the white oak species, this plant can be either a bushy shrub or creeping vine, depending on the moisture content of the soil. In California, the west coast variety of poison oak is ubiquitous and shrubby, but in British

"Where butterflies land, do not place your hand..." a saying that refers to the butterfly's habit of seeking protection on the leaves of poisonous plants.

Columbia, it takes on a more vine-like character. Poison oak, like its cousin poison ivy, has three usually glossy leaves that remind us of oak, but unlike its cousin, the leaves turn scarlet in the fall. Poison oak prefers to hide in shady places and that makes it the least dangerous of the evil triumvirate, but the "do not touch" rule still applies.

• Poison Ivy

This ubiquitous and dangerous weed (*T. radicans* and *T. rydbergii*) is not an ivy but a woody vine with a remarkable ability for subterfuge. The plant is common to Canadian forests but is able to disguise itself with remarkable efficiency. It can be a 4 metre high shrub, a low groundcover or a tree climber with lateral shoots that resemble limbs. It can be so prevalent in forests that it becomes the dominant species and you will not see it for the trees. It can turn itself into a lush bower that beckons the unwary to step off the beaten path for a peek into its vine-draped, shady recesses. But stay on the path, pilgrim, or as the Coasters' song goes, *you are going to need an ocean—of calamine lotion.*

Facts

If lost in the forest and seeking sustenance, do not consume acorns; they will cause you intestinal grief. Also, do not consume a whole apple, apricot or wild cherry; the seeds and pits contain toxic chemicals and will cause you even worse grief.

To produce the Sunday edition of the *New York Times* requires the destruction of around 63,000 trees.

- ### Poison Sumac

Coming into contact with poison sumac (*T. vernix*) is tantamount to having met the devil. It produces the same urushiol as poison ivy, but so much more that the substance fairly oozes from the leaves, fruit and bark. Thankfully, unlike its harmless cousins the staghorn and smooth sumacs that favour dry ground, this monster lurks in swampy areas. Most people encounter this devil when it turns scarlet during autumn, and foragers cannot resist adding the vibrant leaves and fruit to their living rooms or Thanksgiving dinner tables. Of course, the leaves never liven up the living room and Thanksgiving dinner is canceled owing to the host being incapacitated by puss-oozing ulcers.

Urushiol is a resinous oily allergen with a propensity to stick to clothing, gloves, clothes, pets, garden tools and your furniture. Touching poisonous plants with bare hands will spread urushiol to faces, arms and anywhere else the hands touch. Gloves offer protection, but you have to remove the gloves with one bare hand and if your nose happens to itch and needs scratching...well, you get the picture. Urushiol causes the body to produce histamines that rush to the contact points and cause redness and swelling, or what doctors call contact dermatitis. Depending on the amount of urushiol the victim has contacted, the rash can be either slight or severe with pustules and lesions. The rash can appear in hours or days after the contact event and can last up to six weeks. Severe cases are usually treated with cortisone to suppress the immune system, and that is dangerous because it may allow other infections to invade the body.

If you are planning a trip into a forest area, do yourself a favour and memorize pictures of these poisonous plants. If you take along a dog, do not let it wander about in the forest because it may bring back a present you do not want. If you even suspect you have wandered into a bad patch, grab some dish detergent or alcohol and scrub affected areas immediately. Detergent is the key—ecofriendly soaps that contain no detergents will only spread the urushiol and compound the problem. Remove and wash suspect clothes immediately and do not touch them with bare hands.

Note: If you are travelling to a tropical country, remember that our Canadian contact poison plants have tropical relatives that produce urushiol: pistachio, cashew and mangos.

• TREE-OF-HEAVEN

This tree (*Ailanthus altissima*) is more like a weed and likes the dark, damp corners of gardens. To some gardeners it serves a purpose as camouflage for hard-to-work sections since its tendency to sucker from the roots will raise a thicket of green in no time. Problems arise when the new thicket goes to flower or you try to cut down the little jungle—both the pollen and the sap of tree-of-heaven are potent allergens. Do your kids suffer an eye inflammation called conjunctivitis every summer? Look to this plant as the cause, and if you are of a mind to cut the Hydra beast down, wear a mask and avoid exposing any part of your body.

Toxic Weeds

Every summer, thousands of Canadians will contact hospitals, poison control centres and veterinarians to report the ingestion of suspect plant material by children and pets. Pets and children are attracted by colour to flowers and associate pleasant smells with food. It is a dangerous situation, because almost all gardens contain plants, flowers and weeds with toxic abilities. Here is a list.

- VIRGINIA CREEPER

  This fast-growing vine is everywhere in Canada as an ornamental in gardens and roaming in the wild. In the wild, Virginia creeper (*Parthenocissus quinquefolia*) is often confused with poison ivy, but brushing up against this vine will not give you terminal itch, and if you happen to ingest any it will leave you with no more than an upset stomach. Not so for your pets—any Virginia creeper ingestion will spell doom for the little guys. Its sap contains significant amounts of oxalic acid, a chemical their small bodies are unable to process. If you have this vine growing in your garden or patio, keep it high and out of reach of cats and dogs.

- BUTTERCUP

  This yellow flower (*Ranunculus* spp.) is the one small children used to hold under chins of their playmates to see if they like butter. This peculiar childhood pastime is actually a hand-me down custom from more ancient and spookier times when flowers of wolfbane, a close relative of the buttercup, got held under the chins of people suspected of being lycanthropes, or werewolves. If the flower cast a yellow shadow, it meant the suspect only needed a shave and was not a werewolf. Classified a noxious weed in most provinces, the flower contains alkaloids like del-phinin, an allergen if rubbed on the skin and a poison if consumed. It will not kill a child, but it will cause mortality in livestock. If you keep a horse, pay special attention to pasture and paddocks.

- LILY OF THE VALLEY

  Sadly, this groundcover (*Convallaria majalis*) with the sweet-smelling flowers is an invasive weed and extremely dangerous to small children and pets. "Something that smells so good must be tasty" is the thought that has legions of small tasters bundled off to hospitals and veterinarians every summer. The sap of lily of the valley contains glycosides and saponins that may cause grave injury to small fry, so watch them closely when in the garden.

- DATURA, OR JIMSONWEED

  Contrary to popular belief, this member of the Nightshade family is not confined to southern U.S. states and can be found growing in the southern areas of most Canadian provinces. Jimsonweed (*Datura stramonium*) is very dangerous to small children and pets. It has attractive flowers that look and smell scrumptious. If you think your child or pet has ingested any jimsonweed, get them to the hospital fast because the seeds contain hallucinogenic alkaloids that can kill.

- POISON HEMLOCK AND WATER HEMLOCK

  These two members of the Apiaceae family, which includes carrots, parsley, caraway and parsnip, are both deadly. Poison hemlock (*Conium maculatum*) is a European native that earned fame as the poison used to execute the philosopher Socrates in ancient Greece. It grows in southern areas of most Canadian provinces, and prefers a dry terrain near ditches, alongside railway tracks and in woodland areas. Water hemlock (*Circuta douglasii*) is confined to Canada's east coast provinces and is found in swampy areas, drainage ditches and the far recesses of freshwater lakes.

Both contain deadly toxins and, though closely related, they are different. Poison hemlock contains an alkaloid called coniine, which has a chemical structure resembling nicotine, while water-hemlock contains cicutoxin, a powerful nerve disrupter that will cause ascending paralysis and an excruciating death should you happen to consume just one bite of a root and fail to get immediate medical attention. This tragedy has occurred many times, since both genus of weeds look amazingly like wild carrot, or Queen Anne's lace, and they may or may not have similar roots. People who forage for wild edibles should be especially careful not to confuse wild carrot with these incredibly potent look-a-likes, or it may be their last forage.

Note: The poison plants listed above are invasive weeds. Other dangerous garden plants not classified as weeds are in the next chapter, Monsters in the Garden.

• PURPLE LARKSPUR
Plants with magnificent flowers can be deadly. Purple larkspur, the renegade, weedy version of the garden-variety delphinium, looks and smells wonderful and is almost irresistible to cattle and horses. Larkspur is a member of the Ranunculaceae, or Buttercup, family and contains the same alkaloid poison that is similar to the aconitum found in monkshood or wolfbane. In Canada, larkspur comes in two forms, the tall (*Delphinium glaucum*), found in the Rocky Mountains and central BC, and the low (*D. bicolor*), found almost everywhere else. Both like open meadows and fields where cattle and horses pasture and where hay is grown. While special attention to invasive weeds is usually given to grazing land, hayfields are often overlooked, and seeds of the larkspur may become mixed with baled hay and cause deadly problems to livestock.

- MONKSHOOD, *AKA* ACONITUM OR WOLFBANE

There are around 250 species of this plant (*Aconitum* spp.) and almost all pack a lethal wallop. The poison is called "psuedaconitine" and it so deadly that the ancient Japanese and Chinese used it to coat arrowheads for hunting and warfare. In medieval Europe, this plant was used as a poison to dispatch wolves, earning one of its common names, wolfbane. The name monkshood comes from the cowl shape of the attractive flower. Many gardeners throw caution to the wind and plant monkshood in their gardens, while some gardeners plant it without knowing its dark potential. Delphinium and monkshood are available at most garden centres and both sport stunning flowers. In the wild, monkshood leaves and flowers are a grave threat to grazing cattle and horses—they seem to become addicted and will munch away until they die.

While munching leaves and flowers is not usually something people do, the root of the monkshood plant so resembles horseradish that mistakes made by foragers can lead to tragedy.

In the summer of 2004, rising Canadian film star André Clarence Nobel was on a visit to his native Newfoundland when he was treated by friends to a foragers' dinner of wild mushrooms, wild vegetables and roast moose and wild horseradish sauce. Sounds yummy, and probably was until the mistake raised its ugly head. A tingling in the mouth is the first symptom; it begins a few minutes after ingesting acontine. In 10 or 15 minutes, that tingling feeling spreads to the extremities, followed by sweats, vomiting, stomach cramps and death. There is no antidote, and only a spoonful ended a promising film career.

Note: Wear gloves while working in the garden, especially around delphiniums and monkshood. If small children and pets frequent your flower garden, do not plant any poison species.

- Sᴛ. Jᴏʜɴ's Wᴏʀᴛ
This introduced perennial invasive weed (*Hypericum perforatum*) is a threat to livestock in southern areas of Canada. Its flower contains oil glands that produce a photoactive chemical called hyperforin that may cause all manner of problems in livestock including death. The bright yellow flowers have five petals spotted with oil glands that look like tiny, translucent windows. A hybridized version of this plant, *H. moserianum*, commonly called goldflower, is used as a groundcover plant in Canadian gardens and is no threat to curious children, pets or livestock.

- Nɪɢʜᴛsʜᴀᴅᴇ
Related to potatoes, tomatoes and eggplants, this weedy vine has become confused with *Atropa belladonna*, the deadly nightshade indigenous to Europe. It is not the same plant; the berries of our climbing black or hairy nightshade (*Solanacum americanum*) are only mildly poisonous, while those of true deadly nightshade are fatal if ingested. But even "mildly poisonous" can mean a trip to the hospital or vet for small fry, so keep the garden clear of this midnight rambler.

- Fɪᴇʟᴅ Hᴏʀsᴇᴛᴀɪʟ, ᴏʀ Sɴᴀᴋᴇ Gʀᴀss
(*Eǫᴜɪsᴇᴛᴜᴍ ᴀʀᴠᴇɴsᴇ L.*)
A perennial native, this weed prefers poorly drained soils along rail tracks and in open woods, hay-fields and roadside ditches. In hayfields, it becomes a problem when mixed with baled hay because of extreme toxicity to livestock, especially horses.

When first introduced in Europe, tomatoes got a bum rap because of the plants' resemblance to deadly nightshade. In England and other parts of Europe, people somehow became so convinced the tomato was poison that it became associated with witches and devils. The Germans called tomatoes "wolf peaches." In the 18th century, the tomato was scientifically named *Lycopersicon esculentum* and the bum rap continued, since the Latin means "edible wolf peach." Little wonder the tomato did poorly when it arrived in Canada, with most people thinking it a poison right up until Italian immigrants began arriving in the 1870s. However, after one taste of the Italians' bolognese sauce, Canadians forgot about poison plants and have been digging into tomatoes with gusto ever since.

FACTS

(Courtesy of the Nature Institute)

Weed seed resources for birds are reduced in glyphosate-resistant beet production.

Experimental crosspollination between transgenic herbicide-resistant canola and wild field mustard led to highly fertile, herbicide-resistant wild field mustard.

Conventional, certified canola seed lots were contaminated with genetically engineered seeds.

Herbicide-resistant canola volunteers are still detected after 10 years of stringent control.

Monarch butterfly larvae exposed to anthers from *Bt* corn consumed less and had less weight gain than their colleagues who weren't exposed to the anthers.

Herbicide-resistant soybean plants were shorter, had less chlorophyll and lower weight and demonstrated a proclivity towards stem splitting at high temperatures.

Wild sunflowers with the transgene for *Bt* toxin produced more seeds than normal wild sunflowers.

Glyphosate-resistant sugar beets became more susceptible to root rot when sprayed with glyphosate.

Tomatoes engineered for flavonol enrichment had altered levels of at least 15 other substances.

MONSTERS IN
THE GARDEN

It is the nightmare of all Canadian mothers, the disease of the rusty nail: lockjaw. Viewed through a microscope, those dangerous bacteria resemble stickmen with tennis rackets; funny looking, if not for their terrible mission. They are of the genus *Clostridium*, the devil's brigade of bacterium, the bad guys of the invisible world with weapons that modern militaries spend billions trying to emulate: botulism, gas gangrene, diphtheria, whooping cough and the mother and gardener's nemesis, tetanus. These little guys are mean as sin and amazingly resilient. In their vegetative state they are susceptible to air and heat, but they have a trick to counter both: the tiny tennis racket. *Clostridium tetani* lives in the guts of animals, and as the bacterium matures that little tennis racket becomes a spore, separates like a seed and exits through feces. The feces dry and the spores take to the air and travel everywhere. They are on your skin, in your bed, on your clothes—you name it and clostridium spores are there and waiting for a home.

That is weird enough, but it gets weirder, because the bacteria itself does not cause disease; like all assassins they carry weapons that fire bullets called neurotoxins. *C. tetani* fires a bullet called "tetanospasmin," a projectile so lethal that 175 billionth of a gram will have you pushing up daisies. However, that is not the weird part—what is weird is the spot the tiny assassins target: the nervous system, a place where the bacterium cannot travel. Nobody knows why it targets the nerves; it serves the bacterium no purpose other than to cause its host an excruciating expiration.

In Canada's early days, gardening was a gentleman's game, but no gentleman dug in the soil since a cut finger meant a horrible death from the dreaded lockjaw or gangrene. Still, one has to eat something besides potatoes, squash, corn and apples, so the wealthy employed expendables to work the deadly soil: cashiered servicemen, convicts and men considered useless to the community. These expendables died in great numbers, and the wealthy soon ran short of help and sent for English gardeners, the fellows who knew the many secrets of keeping themselves and their masters safe from evils in the soil. They came in droves and their secrets soon had them graduating from expendable to indispensable. English gardeners grew herbs to counter rampant tuberculosis and they sorted ergot sclerotic from grain to prevent dementia and gangrene. In cities like Halifax, Montreal and York (later Toronto), long, dreary winters were endured with occasional seasonal dinner parties to brighten the days. These parties always featured prize specimens of the English gardeners' craft: parsnips, peas, pears and rhubarb, and tropical fruit if the host could afford a conservatory.

English gardeners commanded high wages and if their employer returned to Britain, they sold their services to the highest bidder. A few became wealthy and they owed their good fortune to the tiny monsters that felled so many lesser men. What was their secret to prevent lockjaw and gangrene? What did those English gardeners know or do that so many unfortunate locals did not?

They knew to wear gloves—to not wear any gloves while working a garden is to court disaster from the bacterial spore that causes tetanus, or lockjaw.

Clostridium spores are everywhere and waiting for a home—*C. tetani* kills a half million people annually around the globe, but only a few Canadians have

died since the 1940s when our government initiated a national vaccination program to sensitize citizens against the toxin. Notably successful, it brought *Clostridium* infections to almost a standstill. However, owing to lax government policies regarding immigrant vaccinations, *Clostridium* infections are on the rise all over Canada. In 2008, there were over 7000 cases of whooping cough and in that same year dozens were infected with tetanus—four gardeners succumbed to the disease on Vancouver Island alone.

C. tetani spores are in the air we breathe, on our beds, skin, food and cooking utensils, but mostly they are in the soil. Contrary to popular belief, they have no affinity for rusty nails; the nails are usually outside, dirty and cause a puncture wound that injects the omnipresent bacterial spores. *C. tetani* is anaerobic and needs a deep wound void of oxygen to survive; if you cause yourself that type of wound, get to a hospital for a booster shot. Forget what you heard about boosters being good for 10 years and remember those four unfortunate gardeners on Vancouver Island. Be wise and wear your gloves.

On a slightly brighter note, if that is possible when dealing with monsters in the garden, there are the sneezers, those invisible monsters that attack every spring and make most of us miserable. To understand hay fever and how to control it, one needs a minor understanding of human physiology. Mold spores, pollen and other allergens are everywhere, and they are so tiny they easily enter the bloodstream. Once in, they are tagged as invaders by an immune system that works on the principle of "fool me once, shame on you; fool me twice, shame on me." Not wanting to be shamed, the immune system is ripe and ready with custom-designed antibodies for the next time it encounters the tagged invader. When that occurs, antibodies bind to mast cells that contain histamines and poof, all hell can break loose depending how many antibodies the immune system produced. In most people, the numbers are low and the reaction is no more than a runny nose and the odd sneeze. However, around five million Canadians have an overactive immune system, and reactions can be debilitating and require therapy. There is nothing weird about it—a stranger enters town and the gatekeeper calls out the police. What is weird is that so few allergy sufferers know the identity of the culprits causing their discomfort, their monsters in the garden.

Ahhh-choo, and in very early spring that sneeze is usually caused by tree pollen and mold spores freed from their leafy winter tomb. The wind dries and blows the leaves, allowing mold spores and pollen grains to enter the air we breathe. There's not a lot we can do about that except rake leaves in autumn before the snow flies, only you would have to get your whole block behind the project to have any real effect. What would really help is not to be around the culprits. All trees release pollen into the air, but five trees release far more than others do: birch, alder, poplar, willow and horse chestnut. Of these, birch is the worst—an esti-mated 20% of hay fever suffers are sensitive to its pollen. If you are landscaping, avoid installing any of the big five sneezers. You will be doing yourself and the entire neighbourhood a favour.

FACTS

Humans breathe in mold spores every day. That is not usually a problem because the immune system dispenses with the spores; however, some asthmatics and people with degraded immune systems may suffer an infestation called aspergillosis that requires immediate medical attention.

Contrary to popular belief, pollen grains from golden rod do not cause a reaction in hay fever suffers; the golden rod grains are sticky and depend on birds and bees for transmission. Golden rod got its undeserved reputation because it flowers at the same time as one of the weirdest monsters lurking about the garden, *Ambrosia artemisiifolia*, the not-so-benign common ragweed. "*Ambrosia artemisiifolia*"—such a lovely name for a plant that creates rhinal havoc around the globe. There are over 40 varieties of ragweed around the globe and they will live in almost any environment—hot, cold, dry, wet—and once in there is no showing them the door. Cut them down and they grow back in a week, pull them out by the roots and you have a problem, because the things will release their pollen anyway unless you burn them, and burning things has become inexpedient in most of Canada. Uprooting also poses a risk of skin contact resulting in a latent hyper-sensitivity to the beast. You may recall in the introduction my mentioning the scythe; it is the instrument of choice for eradicating ragweed, but after the reap you must machine mow every three weeks without fail or the monster will return.

Why is *A. artemisiifolia* such a monster? It is the numbers of pollen grains the plant is able to produce. Mature ragweed plants can release over a billion grains over a season. The weed is everywhere and almost 30% of Canadians are sensitive to its pollen. There is nowhere to hide from the beast, and with global warming boosting atmospheric carbon dioxide, it will only get worse. If you are a sufferer, know your enemy and patrol the neighbourhood for signs of the monster. If you find any, get a neighbour you are not particularly fond of to remove them—and remind the neighbour to wear gloves.

Flower gardens are especially inviting to young children and pets, because they are mystical places of visual splendour and inviting smells. Unfortunately, all children and pets are born to explore, and all those bright colours and wonderful smells invite tasting. A nibble will usually not cause any damage, but some toxic plants and flowers taste as good as they smell—and that can be trouble. Cocoa mulch smells terrific and does a good job, but it's loaded with enough of the chemical theobromine to seriously harm dogs and cats. The berries of the chokecherry bush taste good, only the seeds are deadly and have killed children. Baneberry, delphinium and larkspur all contain an alkaloid that will cause severe distress after only a nibble. Elderberries are nice, but if the fruit is unripe, ingesting a few dozen will have your kid in the hospital. Puppies must be watched extra carefully in the garden because their curiosity will have them chewing on almost everything. Weird as it may be, most gardeners have no idea what toxic plants inhabit their bit of heaven. For your erudition, here is a list of toxic plants common to Canadian gardens courtesy of the Children's Hospital of Eastern Ontario:

Toxic Garden Plants

FLOWERS

Azalea (*Azalea indica*)

Bleeding Heart (*Dicentra ormosa*)

Calla Lily (*Zantedeschia aethiopica*)

Carnation (*Dianthus caryophyllus*)

Castor-Oil Plant (*Ricinus communis*)

Chinese or Japanese Lantern (*Physalis*)

Clematis

Crocus (*Colchicum autumnale*)

Daffodil (*Narcissus*)

Delphinium

Foxglove (*Digitalis purpurea*)

Gladiola (the bulb)

Hyacinth (*Hyacinthus orientalis*)

Iris
Jonquil (*Narcissus*)
Lily of the Valley (*Convallaria*)
Morning Glory (*Ipomaea tricolour*)
Narcissus
Oleander (*Nerium oleander*)
Pansy (seeds; *Viola tricolour*)
Peony (root; *Paeonia officinalis*)
Primrose (*Primula*)
Sweet Pea (*Lathyrus odoratus*)
Sweet William (*Dianthus barbatus*)

UNIDENTIFIED WILD MUSHROOMS

All mushrooms should be considered toxic until identified by a mycologist.

VEGETABLES

Potato (green patches found on tubers and any above-ground part; *Solanum*)
Rhubarb (leaves; *Rheum*)
Tomato (greens; *Lycopersicon*)

HEDGES AND BUSHES

Black Locust (*Robinia pseudoacacia*)
Buckthorn (*Rhamnus cathartica*)
Cherry Laurel (*Laurocerasus officinalis*)
Daphne (*Daphne mezereum*)
Elderberry (not berries; *Sambucus*)
Horse Chestnut (*Aesculus hippocastanum*)
Hydrangea
Laburnum (*Laburnum anagyroides*)
Privet (*Ligustrum vulgare*)
Virginia Creeper (*Parthenocissus quinquefolia*)

This list features the most common toxic garden plants; it is by no means comprehensive. Also, keep in mind the words "castor bean tree," as they equate perfectly to a monster in the garden. I think no one in their right mind should plant this tree, but lots do because it grows quickly. Never mind that the pods from this tree harbour seeds that contain the chemical toxin ricin, one of the deadliest poisons on the planet. Both kids and dogs find chewing castor pods almost irresistible and every year a few more end up pushing up daisies because some homeowner is too lazy to rake up the pods or to remove the monster in the garden.

The day is perfect, summer has finally arrived and the garden looks cool and inviting. The young woman places her two toddlers along with their newly acquired puppy onto a blanket where she can keep an eye on them. She settles into a chair with a book and a tall glass of lemonade. A few pages into the book she falls asleep, only to be awakened an hour later by a nightmarish scream. The kids, where are the kids? They are not difficult to find as both are yelling their heads off. She is relieved to find them okay and then is angry over the mess they made of her flowers. Then she sees the puppy. The little guy is drooling and running in circles. She picks him up and looks into his eyes—pupils dilated and he seems unable to focus. She knows what has happened: while she napped, the puppy got busy sampling flowers. She has a horrible thought; curious puppies are very much like small children. What if her kids had sampled along with the puppy and what flowers will hurt them?

This scenario is replayed hundreds of times every season, and while children and pets usually recover after a quick trip to the hospital or the veterinarian, these episodes are best avoided by not mixing children and pets with poisonous plants and flowers.

FACTS

In the U.S., poison control centres receive more than 60,000 calls annually regarding plant poisonings, 85% of which concern small children. Although there are no statistics available for Canada, one can guesstimate around 6000 calls.

Selenium is a chemical found naturally in soil, especially in the western provinces. It can be taken up by some plants, which then become toxic to both animals and humans. An example of a non-toxic species made poisonous by selenium uptake is locoweed, a native herb common in the West.

Molds

Nobody knows exactly how many species of molds inhabit this planet, but guesstimates put the figure at around 300,000. Molds are everywhere, indoors, outdoors and all the places between. They can survive in cold, hot, dry and wet conditions and will be around when the final cockroach on earth breathes its last.

The most common mold in Canada is the species *Cladosporium herbarum.* Pervasive in soil and rotting organic materials, this mold will attach itself to almost anything given the right conditions of warmth and humidity. In homes, it will infest damp basements, acrylic painted walls, air conditioners, humidifiers and mattresses. Sensitization occurs through the breathing of spores and the dried mycelium, the latter being most common in homes. While normally an allergen and not a pathogen to humans, this mold is dangerous to people with compromised immune systems.

Another pervasive mold species is *Stachybotrys chatarum*, a greenish-black mold most commonly found growing on walls after water damage has occurred. This mold is dangerous and should be removed by scrubbing with detergent, not bleach. Bleach is water based, and although it will remove the coloured spores, some parts of the mold will remain and begin growing again. If a large area becomes infected with this "black mold," call in professionals for removal—the stuff is extremely dangerous.

Aspergillus is another widespread mold with a genus of 185 species, 20 of which are pathogenic to humans with compromised immune systems. This mold infests soils and decaying matter, especially compost piles. Wear a mask when you turn your compost pile, and give the job to someone else if you have a compromised immune system.

While allergies are the most common complaint, some molds can also produce mycotoxins, which are dangerous chemicals that make people seriously ill. One of the most dangerous of these is aflatoxin; it is a cancer-causing mycotoxin produced by the fungi *Aspergillus flavus* and *A. parasiticus* found in corn and peanuts. Large brand-name peanut butter manufacturers go to great lengths to make sure their raw materials are free of the aflatoxin. Smaller peanut butter companies are less fastidious, especially with imported African peanuts. Wise and caring parents will spend a little more on well-known brands of peanut butter and avoid cut-rate bargain varieties.

FACTS

To banish mold from most vegetables and berries, dunk them in hot water for 30 seconds: 52° C for thin-skinned fruit like raspberries and strawberries,

and 60° C for thicker-skins like blueberries and tomatoes.

M-o-l-d, is the correct spelling, not...m-o-u-l-d, which is something kids do with modeling clay. Mildew is mold, a horse of another colour, but still mold.

Mold will not be eradicated by painting over infected areas: mold can eat paint.

Nematodes, *aka* Roundworms

Canada's long winters and short summers make a hostile environment for most dangerous insects and arthropods common to U.S. gardens. In the Canadian north, there are deer, black fly and mosquitoes, while in southerly areas of the country hornets and mosquitoes are the main concerns for gardeners. However, there are also tiny animals lurking in your garden that should be a major concern: nematodes.

Commonly called roundworms, nematodes have been around since the dawn of time. They comprise a phylum with as many as 500,000 species. Roundworms are everywhere—on sea bottoms, in freshwater lakes, on mountains, in valleys, in meadows and in your garden soil. Some of their phylum are "predator nematodes" that are beneficial because they kill soil pests like cutworm, while others, "parasitic nematodes," are pathogens to both plants and animals. "What you cannot see will not hurt you" is an adage that holds no water when it comes to roundworms.

- ROUNDWORM OR ASCARIDS
  Human roundworm infections are common. They are caused by the nematode *Ascaris lumbricoides*,

a rather nasty, heavy-bodied worm that inhabits the intestines of over a billion people around the globe. Its eggs and larvae are in the soil everywhere you dig. They will get on your hands and if you touch your mouth they are off to the races. Dogs are the main carrier, and estimates are that 95% of puppies born in Canada carry the worm infection. Raccoons are another source, so get your puppy dewormed and keep the raccoons out of your garden.

The symptoms of ascariasis (roundworm infection) are cough, shortness of breath, tenderness in the gut, pain, vomiting, diarrhea, blood in stool and the presence of worms in vomit or stool.

- HOOKWORM
  The same symptoms occurring with ascariasis infection, plus itchy rash or skin lesions, could indicate infection by another nematode: the hookworm. Hookworm is another parasitic nematode common to dogs, cats and humans. It takes its name from its pronounced hook shape. Hookworm infects approximately 600 million people globally, and while the infection is not usually fatal, the worm's voracious appetite for blood causes pernicious anemia with great economic cost to developing nations. In Canada, hookworm is chiefly an infection of dogs.

- TRICHINOSIS
  During Canada's formative years, many people were infected with the nematode *Trichinella spirallis*, a tiny worm that infests muscle tissue in pigs and game animals. "Cook it hard" was the byword for wise chefs and mothers across the land. Trichinella wound up in the food supply usually by way of rats—pigs ate the rats, people eat the pigs. The way the nematode larva makes itself at home in

people is interesting: it takes over a muscle cell and genetically programs that cell to create a circulatory rete, a blood-infused placenta. Nowadays the little monster is pretty much under control in Canada and it has become a disease of hunters who undercook game. However, the disease is still rampant in areas of China and Asia—avoid consuming pork in those areas.

- PINWORM
This tiny nematode, sometimes called threadworm, does not live in soil and gets a mention here only because it targets children. Estimates are that one-third of all Canadian children will experience an infection some time in their lives. Pinworm is a "people worm"—we are its only host. They are tiny—females 10 mm, males 3 mm—and inhabit the lower intestines. Females exit the anus of sleeping victims at night to lay eggs in folds of skin around the anus and can be seen with a flashlight. Medication is available to kill mature worm and must repeated in two weeks to break the cycle. The medication must be taken by all family members, while bedding, clothing and toys must be thoroughly washed. Pinworm symptoms are anal or vaginal itching, weight loss, irritability and loss of appetite. Although not a major threat to children's health, pinworms can sometimes block the appendix and cause an attack of appendicitis.

Canadians travelling in tropical countries will often return with a nasty little hitchhiker called *Ancylostoma brazililiense*, a thread-like member of the filarial family of tropical roundworms that cause a disease called cutaneous larval migrans. Dogs infected with roundworm larvae defecate in beach sand, and tourists walk and lay in that sand. The roundworm larvae burrow into the skin, making a snake-like track that is incredibly itchy. Some years ago, Rio de Janeiro replaced the sand on its entire beach because of massive infestation of roundworm larvae. Do not lie in the sand of tropical beaches, and wear flip flops or sandals when walking.

While on the subject of tropical roundworms, I had better mention the other little monsters sometimes encountered by tourists. Yes, I know, they have nothing to do with gardening, but gardeners vacation in out-of-the-way places and it is best to be aware of threats. Loiasis is a disease caused by one of the filarial family of nematodes (thread-like) that infects around six million people mainly in Central Africa. Indigenous people call it loa loa, but if you happen to catch it, your doctor will call it "eye worm" since that is where it lives. The yucky factor gets worse, because infected people get to watch it take up residence, yikes! The symptoms are itchy eyes, blurred vision and a tiny worm inching across your vision.

Other members of the filarial family that may threaten tourists are *Wuchereria bancrofti*, *Brugia malayi* and *Brugia timori*. These worms employ mosquitoes as vectors (carriers) and invade the lymph system of their hosts, where they may cause the disease Elephantiasis. Globally, more than 120 million people carry filarial infection. The transmission by mosquito vector is a grave threat to tourists, who are especially at risk in all countries of Asia, Africa and Central and South America. Take along an insecticide-treated mosquito net for sleeping.

Whipworm is another nematode threat to tourists and infects around 500 million people globally. This worm lives in soil and transmits to people through contaminated vegetables, beans and legumes. It is a diner's nightmare, and travellers should consider where they consume their fresh greens. In Canada, whipworm infects dogs and is sometimes transmitted to children.

Regular deworming of dogs should be as important to owners as the wearing of gloves by gardeners.

Metal Monsters

Canada is a mineral-rich country, and it should come as no surprise that some of them can be in your garden soil. Gold, aluminum and a host of others metals can occur naturally in your garden soil as background minerals and are usually nothing to worry about. However, of concern here are the heavy metals, such as cadmium, lead, nickel, chromium, thallium, zinc and arsenic. You are thinking, "Not in my garden," and you are probably right, but to make sure, have your soil checked by a local soil-testing laboratory.

Soil is contaminated by heavy metals in many ways. Arsenic, at one time the insecticide of choice for apple growers, can saturate soil of old orchards. If your house was built anywhere around the site of an old apple orchard, there is a good chance the levels of arsenic are still high in surrounding soil. All house paints once contained a heavy concentration of lead, and if you live in an old house, flaking paint may have contaminated surrounding soil. Zinc, a commonly used coating to protect metal fencing, can leach and contaminate surrounding soil. Sewage sludge may contain high levels of heavy metals, and although you may not have used any as fertilizer, a former owner of your home might have. You simply cannot know what took place on your ground before you came along—that is why a test is imperative.

A soil test costs around $75 and the peace of mind it affords makes it worth every penny. The testing lab will send you containers and instructions for taking samples; follow these instructions to the letter. Use a plastic implement to gather samples, not a metal shovel, and gather from the depth recommended. When you receive the results, the parts per million can be compared to both federal and provincial guidelines published online.

If a certain metals are found in high amounts, but still at acceptable levels, you have a variety of options. You can amend the soil with plenty of organic matter, limestone, phosphorus and clay, all of which will reduce the pH of the soil, making it less likely crops will take up the heavy metals. If the contamination is very light, you can remediate soil by growing sunflowers, but remember to dispose of them properly, because they will be a biohazard. You can build raised beds or confine your planting to crops that will not take up heavy metals, such as tomatoes, cucumbers, peppers and zucchini, and avoid root and leafy vegetables. Raised beds are your best bet, and if metal contamination is high, make the beds a little higher and use plastic sheeting as a base.

Eight-Legged Monsters

Canada is home to thousands of species of spiders, but only three are dangerous to humans: black widow, brown recluse and house spiders. House spiders can be found in almost every province, while the brown recluse and black widows prefers the warmer, central areas of the nation. You should be acutely aware of these spiders, because most recorded bites occur in gardens. Black widow venom affects the nerves, and bites from recluse and house spiders kill cells in the body. Fatalities are rare, but if you are bitten, get immediate medical attention so rarities can stay the norm.

Psst! Wear your garden gloves!

Bigger Monsters

Raccoons, possums, groundhogs, coyotes, squirrels and rabbits all seem to relish your garden more than your neighbour's. It seems that way, but the truth is your garden is only a stop along the forage trail. The aforementioned animals have adapted to life with humans

and have established food routes, and your garden is just one stop along the way. With this in mind, wise gardeners can make their food stop unappetizing to furry bandits in a variety of ways.

- SQUIRRELS

"Feed the mother and her future generations will forever be at your door." I found this maxim out quite by accident. One blustery winter day, a pair of tiny American grey squirrels appeared at my kitchen window, one black and one grey. The American grey squirrel does not hibernate, and mothers will often bear young late or early during a season. The pair at my window could not have been more than a month old and had probably been driven from their drey (nest) by older siblings after momma failed to return from the daily forage. I wanted to bring them inside, but my wife thought it best to leave them as they looked on death's doorstep and any stress would be fatal. Instead, we provided a box and blanket and opened the window a crack to provide warmth.

Over the next few days, we hand-fed those huddled cuties crushed walnuts and peanut butter. The babies thrived. In spring, the black female went away, but the grey male—we called him Herbie—continued his feeding visits for a time until he too went away (he was probably run over by a car). That winter, the black female returned to our window—burying nuts is probably a learned trait and no one had taught her the skill. We called her Momma, and she had come to show her brood how to survive the winter the only way she knew how.

That was several years ago, and every winter we get Momma and generations of her offspring at our window. Vehicle mortality is high in our city, so there are never that many, and the ones that do appear, including the long-lived Momma, are very well mannered. They line up and sit patiently with their little front feet tucked up in begging mode and are fed one by one with never a grab or bite.

The moral of this little story is, if you happen upon orphaned animals, call your local animal control office and avoid becoming the momma—it is a huge responsibility and is best avoided.

Keeping squirrels out of your garden requires ingenuity—the little cuties will second-guess your every move. Squirrels are natural bandits and take great delight in foiling whatever scheme you devise to thwart their freeloading, especially when it comes to birdfeeders. To stymie the little guys, you must watch them a while, and you will learn their preferred route to your garden. Squirrels like to move about in the treetops, and they will descend from there to your garden like fighter planes. Disrupt their route and 90% of the time they will abandon the dive and head for easier pickings down the road. It could be as easy as cutting a branch near your back fence or one close to your garage or garden shed roof. If that fails, try shooting them and frying up their little carcasses for lunch—I'm just kidding! But if you yell that threat loud enough you might scare them into raiding your neighbour's garden.

Some gardeners lay down coarse mesh to protect flower bulbs, but when I tried that, I got to watch from a window as a squirrel figured out where the screen ended and tunneled in for dinner. Perhaps you could strike a deal with raiding squirrels. "I'll put more seed in the birdfeeder and you leave the garden alone." Try anything,

something might work, and if you find something please let me know.

- RACCOONS

Aside from dogs, raccoons are probably the most adaptable of all small animals. Humans domesticated the dog to be useful but passed on the more practical raccoon owing to its irascibility and nocturnal habits. I sometimes wonder what a world with domesticated raccoons would be like—they are a whole lot smarter than dogs and have paws that are almost hands. Thousands of years of domestication and we have dogs able to lead the blind, herd sheep and fetch the morning paper. Had the raccoon been domesticated instead, they could be leading the blind by the hand, washing dishes, cleaning house and doing the shopping. They like shopping; it is what they do in your neighbourhood vegetable gardens. They know when your tomatoes will ripen and when your neighbour's zucchini will be at its most delectable.

Years ago, I went duck hunting with a group of friends and had occasion to witness the shopping habits of raccoons. We stayed in a cabin that featured a deck and clothesline to hang the day's bag of ducks. That first night, while excusing myself from the poker game to attend the outside loo, I encountered a strange group of thieves on the deck, a mama raccoon and her five kits. The mother, one of the largest raccoons I had ever seen, had dragged a deck chair under the clothesline where the ducks hung. She had climbed aboard the chair so she could reach the ducks, and as I watched, she picked a duck off the line and handed it down to one of her brood, while the others shoved the chair along to the next duck. My presence did not faze her one bit, and she just kept on shopping. Shopping it was, because she was selective and passed on ducks that looked too shot up. It took all my friends and brooms to persuade momma and her bandit kits to leave—grudgingly. Only when she was gone did I truly appreciate her *modus operandi*. The ducks she had passed down had been run into the bush by one of her brood with purpose in mind—knowing she would be caught in the act, momma raccoon had secured her purloined selections against our retrieval.

Show me a dog capable of such thought process and I will eat a can of dog food. Can you guess that I admire the little rascals? I really do, but when they show up at my kitchen window, and they do now and then, I shoo them away because the little guys can carry disease: rabies, leptospirosis, listeriosis, tetanus, tularemia and roundworm.

Make your yard unattractive to raccoons by raking up dropped fruit from trees and securing garbage in steel cans with tight lids. Gardens are another matter, especially if you grow sweet corn, a crop they find hard to resist. A dog is your best protection from raccoon raids on the garden. If you do not have a dog, borrow one for a few nights and the raccoons will cross your garden off their shopping route.

If a dog is not feasible, try motion-sensor lights and place a few ammonia whiffers in strategic spots in the garden. Punch a hole in the lid of a large jar, insert a rag, fill the jar with liquid ammonia and screw on the top. Raccoons have excellent memory and will remember the noxious smell of ammonia for several seasons. Mixing 1 part castor oil with 10 parts of water and lacing the garden perimeter is another odoriferous animal stopper.

- BEARS AND COYOTES
Canada has healthy bear and coyote populations in many towns and cities. Bears and coyotes

are both omnivores and will eat just about anything: ants, mice, rabbits, dogs, cats, berries, sheep, fruit, garbage and your entire vegetable garden. Bears are not particularly smart, but they are gifted with the innate knowledge that "big demands respect." If a bear wants into your vegetable garden, there is not a lot to be done except call 911 and be referred to animal control's voice mail. By the time city bureaucrats get around to your bear problem, the beast has gone and so has all your hard work. I think if a bear ambles into my garden I shall call 911 and tell them a burglar is breaking in, and I will sort out the confusion later. Living in Toronto, I do not expect to find a bear in my garden, but then I never expected to see a coyote trotting across my path.

In the summer months, I am head gardener for a large golf and country club on the outskirts of Toronto. Lots of wildlife live in those secluded acres, and not an early morning passes that does not feature a parade of various animals: deer, raccoons, beaver, martin, mink and of course coyotes. It used to be the coyotes would spot my golf cart long before I saw them and they would just be a blur in the trees. Not any more—now they just lope along, oblivious to my presence. It is a little unnerving, considering they are no longer emaciated little prairie runners. The guys on my golf course are eastern coyotes—immigrants from the prairies who have inbred with wolves and dogs, a genetic mix that has doubled their size and suppressed their fear of man.

Remember Wile E., the coyote in the "Roadrunner" cartoons? The only similarity nowadays is the name, because they certainly are wily. In cities, they will haunt back streets and alleys hunting for cats, dogs and found food—including your tomatoes, zucchini and grapes—hey, they will try anything. If you find one ravaging your garden, yell long and loud and that should scare it off.

- RABBITS

Cute and definitely not monsters, rabbits are still capable of doing monster-like damage to your vegetable and flower garden. Nothing personal—the little guys are just hungry and the stuff in your garden beats nibbling on weeds hands down.

Fencing is the best rabbit deterrent, with 20 centimetres under the ground and 90 centimetres above. If that sounds daunting, try making your crop unappetizing to the little rascals by spraying with denatonium benzoate, the bitterest stuff on the planet. The chemical is safe—it is used in consumer products like rubbing alcohol, nail-biting solution, liquid soaps and antifreeze where as little 10 parts per million will deter human consumption. Denatonium benzoate excels as an animal repellent and is available under the brand names Bitrex or Aversion.

Note: Bitrex and Aversion will repel most animals (it works wonders on deer), but for inexplicable reasons, cats seem to like the stuff.

- GROUNDHOGS, VOLES AND MOLES

Bitrex, Aversion, castor oil, ammonia or shotguns are the recommended cure for rodents in the garden. However, since shooting up the neighbourhood in cities and towns is pretty much out of vogue these days unless you desire to meet the local SWAT squad, the other methods work fine. The trick is to make your garden less attractive than the one down the road—and nothing makes a garden less attractive than a foul taste or smell. The repellents only last a few days and will disappear in the next rainfall, so repeat applications

are necessary. Do not worry about the bitter or odoriferous chemicals showing up in your salad greens—they safely dissipate into the air.

- DEER

Bambi will clean your garden out of flowers or vegetables so fast you will think a tornado has swept through. Golf course gardeners hear many stories of what deer can do to flowers, especially tulips. My favourites involve new clubs and their city landscape designers who insist upon a big show of spring blooms. "What deer? We've been building this place for eight months and no one has seen a trace of deer."

So, into the ground goes the big show. Come spring, just before the grand opening, 10,000 imported Dutch tulips bulbs are up and framing the club-house in a rainbow of colours. "See, no deer. I told you so," says the pleased designer to his worried gardener.

Of course, you already know the story ending—no deer, but the next morning, no tulips. Masters of camouflage and patience, deer will stand in the trees like statues waiting for the right moment to venture forward. Night or day, it matters not, but their usual time for feasting is early morning, just before sunrise.

Fences are a good deterrent, but you will need a high one because they jump like Rudolph. A temporary electric fence works best—deer seem to associate the shock with hornets and will give your garden a wide berth. One strand of wire will suffice, but make sure you insulate properly and use a commercial transformer.

Going online will provide dozens of tips to deter deer, but the best is the electric fence or making your garden fare unappetizing to those lithe and lovely creatures with Bitrex. One nibble sends them bounding off, never to return, and after a few days the stuff dissipates and things are normal again.

FACTS

In Canada, the mushroom *Amanita phalloides*— common name "death cap"—is responsible for many accidental poisonings. The toxin found in this mushroom causes cramping, vomiting, diarrhea and liver and kidney failure. Consuming just one mushroom may cause fatalities to adults, while higher death rates are recorded for children owing to body size.

Of the more than 10,000 mushroom species found in North America, about 200 are poisonous and only around a dozen are deadly poisonous.

There is no antidote for deadly mushroom toxin: you eat, you suffer and die, end of story. Do not forage for wild mushrooms unless accompanied by an expert mycologist.

WEIRD GARDEN INNOVATIONS

S oil is a complex universe of atoms and molecules that are constantly under stress and becoming ionized. An ion is a molecule or atom with an unequal number of negatively charged electrons to positively charged protons, an out of balance atom or molecule. Too many electrons in soil molecules means a positive charge (cation), while too many protons is a negative charge (anion). Ion balance of soil is a measure of fertility; soil scientists call it "cation exchange capacity" or CEC and use it to measure the capacity of ion exchange between soil and soil solutions. It is a handy measurement if you want soil with optimum growing ability, and a device to measure CEC is already in use by farmers. Stuck into the ground, the device sends information to the farmer's computer, from which he or she is able to ascertain the day-by-day health of the soil. In a few years, this device will be available to the home gardener, and guesstimates of soil pH, fertilizer and lime applications will be forever banished. The soil will be in charge and the benefits to home gardeners will be a doubling of crop yield.

The University of California at Berkeley has made great strides in the area of nanotechnology, and that includes devices that operate on the atomic or molecular scale and can read the health of soil. They have also perfected a sensing chip imbedded with thousands of DNA fragments from plant pathogens. Coupled to a laser, this chip will read a cultivated area for invasive diseases, insects and weeds, and alert the farmer or gardener via cell phone. Sensing chips have been around for years, but adapting them with nanotechnology will revolutionize commercial agriculture and home gardening.

The words "urban farmer" are beginning to make sense. City rooftops will soon have the capability to feed vast numbers of residents because urban farmers will arrive at their rooftop gardens knowing exactly what is required for optimum plant health. The benefits in saved labour and crop yields, coupled with the insulation capability of green roofs, will turn our cities into important food producers. However, the reality of large-scale, economically viable green roof food production is still years down the road, and while several installations are already operational in Canada, most are government funded and make little economic sense.

British Columbia's Liberal government recently opened a huge 2.5-hectare roof garden atop the Vancouver Convention Centre that contains over 400,000 plants and grasses. It was a rushed affair to be ready for the 2010 Winter Olympic Games, and there are already reports of leaks and other problems. The City of Toronto has hatched a plan to make green roofs mandatory on all building projects after January 1, 2010. It's an admirable undertaking, but what they will get are rooftops with a thin layer of soil over membrane that will support only small succulent plants—it's good for soaking up rainwater and great for insulation, but short-sighted in that it will do nothing to help feed the masses and only add to the high cost of housing in that city.

Rushing to green has become synonymous with government, and financial and ecological debacles are going to be commonplace on the long road to American energy independence. Canada is already energy independent; we have enough oil and gas, and the country is a net exporter of electricity. Then why do we need all those ugly, bird-killing, expensive

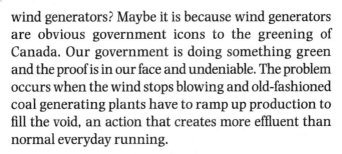

wind generators? Maybe it is because wind generators are obvious government icons to the greening of Canada. Our government is doing something green and the proof is in our face and undeniable. The problem occurs when the wind stops blowing and old-fashioned coal generating plants have to ramp up production to fill the void, an action that creates more effluent than normal everyday running.

Biotechnology is fast opening new paths of opportunity for Canadian farmers who might in the near future grow engineered specialty crops that produce vaccines, antibodies and nutritional supplements, a kind of pharmacy in the field. This technology may also be available to home gardeners and will cause a marked rise in the number of herbalists and do-it-yourself natural healers. TV hawkers might sell grow-it-yourself vitamin kits and Internet sites may appear to assist gardeners in growing exotic pharmaceuticals. Laugh now, but the separation between, food, cosmetics and medicines is disappearing quickly. Food products that claim medicinal and cosmetic benefits have been on supermarket shelves for years and new ones are introduced almost daily: margarines that lower blood cholesterol; bread that scavenges free radicals; rice engineered to provide exotic vitamins or for people allergic to rice; yogurts with new kinds of bacteria to benefit figures and complexions; breakfast cereals to make you regular; and on and on. Biopharmaceutical companies have engineered plants to produce vaccines for various ailments, such as hepatitis B, and are already in the testing stage. There are shampoos, wrinkle creams and drinks to make you strong, and they all are from genetically fiddled plants. It is an unstoppable wave of technology and only time will tell if it benefits or bites mankind in the butt.

Green is eminently desirable for Canada, but good intentions can easily get out of hand as government bureaucrats are rushed to green by legions of media doomsayers. It's a pity, because the way to a greener Canada is not that difficult and only requires a few stops: stop giving foreign companies *carte blanche*, stop dumping toxic substances into the soil, water and atmosphere, and stop selling cheap energy to the Americans. Crank up the price of our energy, and our American friends will do what they do best and invent some new source of power or concentrate on perfecting their present energy technologies. Canada will lose money, but our environment will get a huge break.

Sorry for the rant, but I am still reeling from our federal government's idiotic decision to permit Ontario Hydro to turn Wolf Island, a migratory bird stop in the St. Lawrence River, into a wind farm. Wind farms are a monstrous insult to nature and human sensibilities and if not stopped they will spread like a virus into every windy spot in Canada. Any wind in your backyard?

Hydroponic Kitchen Gardens

In a few years, almost every home will feature an automated, hydroponic vegetable garden. New homes will come with gardens instead of swimming pools—or ingenious combinations of both—and pool servicing will be replaced by a monitoring garden service. The garden man will come on a regular basis to check your sensors and pumps but may arrive anytime sensors indicate a problem.

The garden of the near future will be a fresh food-processing unit integral to the kitchen; herbs, salads and dinner sides will be just a few steps out the back door for everybody. Those small hydroponic units peddled on TV will grow you a tiny assortment of greens; but they are toys compared to what the future holds for kitchen gardeners. No mess, no fuss, as computers and the garden service man will take care of everything. Kitchen gardeners will only have to decide what and

how many items the units will produce: tomatoes, potatoes, carrots, lettuce, radishes—you name it and your unit will provide it. Once you taste the produce, no sane individual would dream of returning to the supermarket for fresh greens and sides. Why wait for the future? With fresh greens already so expensive and steadily rising in price, a hydroponic kitchen unit makes sense now and should pay for its construction in just a few years.

FACTS

Israel has more than 30,000 acres devoted to commercial hydroponics, more than all other countries combined.

Hydroponically grown plants and vegetables are usually more healthy and vigorous than their standard grown counterparts owing to ready availability of nutrients.

Square Fruit and Vegetables

Have you seen square watermelons on supermarket shelves yet? They are a weird innovation in North American markets, but the Japanese have been growing and marketing the fruit for 20 years. A farmer from the island of Shikoku came up with the idea to facilitate shipping. He just grew his melon in glass boxes, and the fruit just naturally assumed that shape. Today, hugely expensive square and pyramid-shaped melons are in markets all over Japan, but are considered fashion food. A few Mexican growers are producing square melons and some Canadian supermarkets are giving them a try, so keep your eyes peeled and be ready for that pleasant shock. If you think them too expensive, grow your own—there is nothing hard about it and instructions are available online.

Grow Bags

Plop down the bag, cut holes for the plants, insert the watering valve and all that's left is deciding what to grow. No muss, no fuss and they take up very little space. It's kind of gardening by numbers, but if space is a problem, they might be your cup of tea. You can suspend grow bags from balcony ceilings or tree branches and cut holes all over the bag. Tomatoes seem to like being aerial and will produce some amazingly large fruit for your troubles. Europeans have used grow bags for ages; city residents will stuff window boxes with the bags, and small patios with sunny corners given over to the bags can grow almost every vegetable.

PLANTING THE GROW BAG

Loosen the soil/compost in the bag by kneading and shaking.

Pierce the base of the bag for drainage and cut out pre-marked holes in the top for plants. If salad greens are the intended crop, cut out a long rectangle.

Position the bag so it forms a slight hump in the middle.

Scoop out soil from holes, carefully insert vegetable plants and pack with scooped soil.

Water well and be sure to label if you are planting multiple bags.

Planting tomatoes directly into a grow bag can turn messy when watering, so cut large holes in the bottoms of the 12" or 14" plastic containers growers use to ship plants. If you buy half-matured vegetable plants you already have this container; if not, ask your nurseryman—he always has

a corner full of them somewhere. Place the plant into the container so the roots poke out. Fill with soil gathered from two X slits in the grow bag. Then, place your containers into the slits, two per bag, making sure the plastic film of the bag fits tightly around the containers. No mess, no fuss and you do not have to use standard grow bags—you can use commercially bagged compost or any compost/soil mixture. Just do not forget to cut the drainage slits in the bottom of the bags.

Automated Fertilizer Systems

These systems have been used by commercial growers for decades, and they are finally available to home gardeners. They attach to your water supply and inject a measured amount of fertilizer into your hose, drip system or sprinkler. Brand-name fertilizers are available in bottle dispensers that attach to the end of a garden hose, and while they bear a slight resemblance to automated systems, there is no comparison when it comes to controlling amounts and formulation. With the automated system, you can use whatever formulation of fertilizer that is right for your plants.

Time Lapse Video Camera

Use a weatherproof video camera to take wide-angle shots of your garden at various times and transmit the video to your computer. You can watch your garden grow, or get an up-close look at raccoons feasting on your lettuce crop.

Misting Towers

A misting tower screwed on your garden hose will produce a delightful cooling mist with many hot weather garden applications, e.g., they cool down the salad greens, keep flying insects at bay, and keep gardeners from swooning in the noonday sun.

Worm Composters

Imagine red worms, thousands of them, every one working to turn your organic waste into castings that will brighten up your garden like nothing else on the planet. These composters look like the normal plastic variety, but they have drawers. You place the worms in the bottom drawer, garbage in the bin on top, and the worms eat their way up, leaving behind a treasure of castings in the lower drawers. I have yet to see one of these in action, but I do like the sound of it, and I will do just about anything for a steady supply of worm castings.

BioBags

Made from corn, these plastic-looking yard bags break down in your composter in only a few days. Stuff them full of leaves and pop them into the composter—how easy is that?

FACTS

(Courtesy of the Food and Agricultural Organization of the United Nations)

Of the roughly a quarter million plant varieties available for agriculture, only 3% are being used for that purpose.

The entire world's food supply depends on around 150 plant species; of these just 12 supply three-quarters of the world's food.

The world's poor depend on plants for as much as 90% of their needs: food, fuel, medicine, transportation and shelter. Approximately 1.4 billion people, mostly resource-poor farmers, use and improve their own crop seeds, which helps

to maintain and enhance the genetic diversity of crops.

Millions of resource-poor farmers eke out a livelihood on small parcels of marginal land in remote mountainous or arid regions. Yet it is estimated that resource-poor farmers produce as much as 20% of the world's food, largely without benefit of modern farm implements and agriculture research.

The majority of the world's resource-poor farmers are women; in some regions, they produce as much as 80% of the food.

WEIRD WEATHER AND CLIMATE CHANGE

Our sun makes weather. Earth is round and the curvature deflects solar radiation, except at the equator, which bakes in direct radiation. The equatorial oceans heat, water evaporates, rises, cools and falls as rain in a relentless cycle. Earth's atmosphere is an extension of those oceans; they feed and propel it, make it calm and angry and govern temperatures. Our atmosphere is a vast ocean, with currents, variable depths, density and weight. Being "light as air" is a misnomer, as the breathing stuff weighs in at 1 kilo per square centimetre, that's 1 ton pressing down on every square foot. They do not call it the air column for nothing—little wonder we have joint problems and walk on two feet. Pity the four-legged animals; big and swayback is no fun.

What is the difference between weather and climate? Weather is simply a disruption of the long-term expectation of what we call the climate. British Columbia residents, for example, expect warm, dry summers with the odd arctic cold snap in winter—that's climate. However, if they get a weeklong downpour in July, that is weather, foul weather. During the summer of 1955, Montreal saw 33 days of temperatures above 30° C, and many residents believed their weather had become climate and blamed American atom bomb testing.

Weather and climate are two distinct fields of study. Meteorologists concern themselves with weather occurring now, and climatologists work with relics of past events: tree rings, sediment cores from ocean bottoms, glaciers, pollen trapped in ice, amber and sedimentary strata in rocks. While divergent in studies, both these fields work towards the same goal: a better understanding of weather events. Weather events are important to gardeners: hail, frost, heavy rain and winds can wipe out weeks of hard work in minutes. The wise gardener is online watching weather reports like a hawk and is prepared for all weather eventualities.

High Winds

If high winds are a constant threat, construct a break on the windward side of the garden. It can be a 1 metre high lattice fence, hay bales or a more permanent row of shrubs. Growing runner beans and peas can be a problem in windy areas. To protect them from wind damage, create tepees from the normal post string trellis, and tie them together with a 1" × 2" ridgepole.

Hail, Frost and Heavy Rain

If any of the above should threaten, the wise gardener is ready with protective netting. Frost netting is handy stuff and widely available. Measure enough to cover your garden, tack the edges to 1 × 2s, secure one end to the ground and roll the netting onto the other 1 × 2. Place 1 × 2 stanchions in the garden to support the net and at the first sign of inclement weather, roll it over the crop. Frost netting can also double as shading for tender crops.

My editor has warned me not to include gardening tips in this book—I am to focus on facts—but you have to know this one. It is for that special tree or shrub that everyone has in the garden—the one that causes you worry when the weatherman predicts abnormally low temperatures. Wrap that special tree in Christmas lights—not the modern LED kind, but the old-fashioned bulb type, the ones that will give off just enough heat to protect that tree.

Cloud Primer

Should gardeners know how to forecast weather? If I thought yes, I could lay out a short course in meteorology, but I think no—that is how local weathermen earn their pay, and we gardeners already have enough on our plate. I suggest you find a good local meteorologist and stick with his or her forecasts.

On second thought, every gardener should know a little something about clouds and lightening. Clouds are usually benign or threatening and can be read like a book, while lightning is a hidden danger to gardeners and is best avoided. Here is a very brief cloud and lightning avoidance primer.

Clouds are either cumulus or stratus; the former is puffed up by rising warm air, the latter is a high-altitude fog created by air that does not rise. Clouds are further divided into four altitudes: towering, high, middle and low.

- Towering clouds can rise to over 25,000 metres and behave badly; these black "hats" often have the Latin word *nimbus* (rain cloud) tacked on so you know not to walk the dog. If you see one of these in the neighbourhood, stay inside.
- High clouds, or alto, are composed of tiny ice crystals and are found at altitudes of 6000–9000 metres. They are divided into three types: cirrus (sometimes called "mare's tails") look like wispy streaks of white in a blue sky; cirrocumulus (sometimes called a "mackerel sky") look rippled and wavy; and cirrostratus, which are thin, high-altitude gossamer sheets composed of ice crystals and are responsible for halos around the sun or moon.
- Middle clouds are divided into alto or cumulus and are found at altitudes of 2000–6000 metres. Altostratus are dense sheets of grey but can

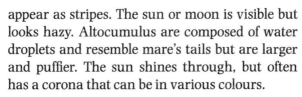
appear as stripes. The sun or moon is visible but looks hazy. Altocumulus are composed of water droplets and resemble mare's tails but are larger and puffier. The sun shines through, but often has a corona that can be in various colours.

- Low clouds begin at around 1800 metres and have three types: stratus, nimbo and strato. Stratus is a thick grey fog covering the entire sky and is responsible for drizzling rain. These clouds form when there is little or no vertical movement of air. Nimbostratus are rain clouds; dark and ominous, they sometimes touch the ground. Nimbostratus are actually middle clouds with low bases and occurring precipitation but can belong to any grouping because vertical extension can be massive. Stratocumulus are irregular masses of various shades of grey spread out in layers. No rain comes from these clouds, but they bear watching because they sometimes fuse into nimbostratus and cause sudden downpours.

- Cumulonimbus are the ones to watch. Bases may touch the ground and updrafts rise to over 25,000 metres. High winds aloft can sometimes cleave their tops so they resemble a blacksmith's anvil. Thunderstorms and tornadoes spawn from these clouds. They also produce positive lightning strikes, so do not walk the dog.

- Cumulus are fine weather clouds, unless they come together and form a cumulonimbus, but that does not happen often since the average lifespan of a cumulus cloud is only 15 minutes.

Outdoor Precautions During Lightning Events

To help you out, here are a few tips from Environment Canada. Start by learning the 30-30 Rule. Take appropriate shelter when you can count 30 seconds or less between the lightning's flash and the thunder. Remain sheltered for 30 minutes after the last thunderclap.

- Keep a safe distance from tall objects such as trees, hilltops and telephone poles.
- Avoid projecting yourself above the surrounding landscape. Seek shelter in low-lying areas such as valleys, ditches and depressions—but be aware of flooding.
- Stay away from water. Do not go boating or swimming if a storm threatens, and get to land as quickly as possible if on the water. Lightning can strike the water and travel some distance from its point of contact. Do not stand in puddles even if you are wearing rubber boots.
- Stay away from objects that conduct electricity, such as tractors, golf carts, golf clubs, metal fences, motorcycles, lawnmowers and bicycles.
- Take off shoes with metal cleats.
- Avoid being the highest point in an open area. Swinging a golf club or holding an umbrella or fishing rod can make you the tallest object and a target for lightning. If you are on a level field far from shelter and feel your hair stand on end, lightning may be about to hit you. Kneel on the ground immediately with your feet together, place your hands on your knees and bend forward. Do not lie flat. The object here is to make as small a target as possible.
- You are safe inside a vehicle during lightning, but do not park near or under trees or other tall objects that may topple during a storm. Be aware of downed power lines that may be touching your car. You will be safe inside the car, but you may receive a shock if you step outside.
- In a forest, seek shelter in a low-lying area under a thick growth of small trees or bushes.
- Keep alert for flash floods, sometimes caused by heavy rainfall, if taking shelter in a ditch or low-lying area.

- If you are in a group in the open, spread out and keep people several metres apart.

Indoor Precautions During a Storm

- Before the storm hits, disconnect electrical appliances, including radios, televisions and computers. Do not touch them during the storm.
- Do not go outside unless absolutely necessary.
- Keep away from doors, windows, fireplaces and anything that will conduct electricity, such as radiators, stoves, sinks and metal pipes. Keep as many walls as possible between you and the outside.
- Do not handle electrical equipment or telephones. Use battery-operated appliances only.

FACTS

Lightning may strike up to 35 kilometres from a storm cloud into clear weather. If you can see the storm on the horizon, lightning can still be a threat.

Official figures put annual lightning fatalities at six to 10 in Canada. However, each year lightning seriously maims and injures hundreds and those go mostly unreported.

Climate Change

On maps of the world, Canada looks massive and reaches right up into the arctic fringe. However, as most of our people huddle within a few hundred kilometres of the cross-country rail system, the geographic reality is that Canada more accurately resembles a longer version of Chile, the country in South America. Canada's north, while pristine and beautiful, is a mostly inhospitable place—a nice place to visit, but you would not want to live there. The winters are harsh and black fly and mosquitoes rule the brief summers; on the other hand, our vast north is a veritable treasure trove of resources and an irresistible lure to large corporations poised to take advantage of current warming trends.

Nowadays, because of global warming, James and Hudson Bays are nearly ice-free year-round, and commercial shipping to the very gates of the Northwest Passage has shown a marked increase. If the warming trend continues, the passage will become another St. Lawrence Seaway, and the north will see an economic surge never before experienced in Canada. New rail lines will head north from prairie cities to terminals in newly constructed ports, and cities will spring up almost overnight.

All across Canada's near arctic, hundreds of prospected viable mine sites sit waiting for the day the ice melts, and the Canadian government is betting millions that day will arrive soon. The infrastructure of existing arctic communities is being bolstered and new communities and ports are in the works.

A lot is resting on what is commonly referred to as global warming. The world is heating up, an undeniable fact with repercussions—some areas of the globe will suffer from changing weather patterns and rising water levels, while others, like Canada, will reap huge benefits.

To better comprehend how global warming might work, an understanding of where our weather originates is necessary. Weather begins at the equator; the sun beats straight down, heating water and sending vapour into the air like a mighty fountain with half going north and half south. Hot air rising into cool cannot hold onto the water vapour and it begins to rain until the water vapour is exhausted. Dry air is heavy and down it comes onto an area of the Pacific Ocean between latitudes

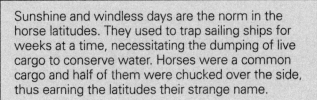

Sunshine and windless days are the norm in the horse latitudes. They used to trap sailing ships for weeks at a time, necessitating the dumping of live cargo to conserve water. Horses were a common cargo and half of them were chucked over the side, thus earning the latitudes their strange name.

30° and 35° north and south—commonly referred to as the "horse latitudes," a place bereft of weather.

The earth's rotation causes horse latitude air to move east into North America, and residents enjoy fine weather until northeast-moving low-pressure cells muscle in and cause precipitation. Without those low-pressure cells, Canada would have no weather and would be like the Sonora region in the U.S. southwest and northern Mexico: a desert. The horse latitudes cause desertification of lands right around the globe: the Sonora, Sahara and Kalahari in the Northern Hemisphere, the Atacama and Australian deserts in the south. Never heard of the Atacama Desert? That is an area of high plateau on the wrong side of the Chilean Coastal Mountain range and the driest place on the globe—so dry the soil has become sterile. If travel is your thing, mark the Atacama off your list. It is a place of ultimate desolation and the saddest place on the planet. However, all that could change if horse latitude air took longer to become dry. A few degrees of warmer air at high altitudes north and south of the equator could translate into a shift in the desert-causing horse latitudes. Nobody knows what effect that might have on global weather patterns; it could amount to nothing, or it could deprive completely new areas of normal precipitation, or it could even rain in the driest place on earth: the Atacama Desert.

If you go around the globe, you will find no sea level rise anywhere. But they need the rise, because if there is no rise, there is no death threat. They say there is nothing good to come from a sea-level rise, only problems, coastal problems. If you have a temperature rise, if it's a problem in one area, it's beneficial in another area. But sea level is the real bad guy, and therefore they have talked very much about it. But the real thing is, that it doesn't exist in observational data, only in computer modeling.

—Dr. Nils-Axel Morner, noted climatologist

FACTS

The lowest temperature recorded in Canada was –63° C at Snag, in the Yukon Territory, on February 3, 1947.

The idea of naming hurricanes originated with an Australian weather forecaster who decided to name them after politicians he despised.

A hurricane can drop up to 20 billion tons of rainwater per day.

Global Warming

The Earth has been warming and cooling in a cyclical manner since before the Quaternary Period ice age ended 10,000 years ago. Cyclical warming and cooling are the tail end of that period, a time when the Earth froze, melted and froze again. From the 1st century to the 13th, in what climatologists call "the medieval warm period," our world enjoyed a warming trend. From the 13th century to the middle of the 19th in what climatologists call a "mini Quaternary" or "little ice age," the Earth cooled. In Europe during the little ice age, rivers

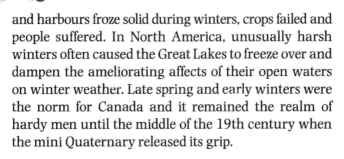

and harbours froze solid during winters, crops failed and people suffered. In North America, unusually harsh winters often caused the Great Lakes to freeze over and dampen the ameliorating affects of their open waters on winter weather. Late spring and early winters were the norm for Canada and it remained the realm of hardy men until the middle of the 19th century when the mini Quaternary released its grip.

Warming is a whole lot better than cooling, but too many people wanting too many things can throw logs onto the fire, causing the pot to boil instead of simmer. With the Earth warming and crop production assured, mankind turned to making consumer goods. Steam-driven machines enabled factories to produce goods faster and cheaper, but feeding the machines required coal, and the world should have learned from the experience. The Industrial Age choked cities with pollution, and coal-burning fireplaces only added to the mess. In the winter of 1952, residents of London, England, awoke to a cold snap and lit up a million fireplaces. The temperature inversion that caused the cold snap trapped carbon emissions and thousands died. Lesson learned, because in 1954 Britain passed the Clean Air Act, which outlawed coal-burning fireplaces and required industries to rein in their polluting ways and move to the countryside.

Most developed countries followed Britain's example and their cities could breathe again. However, scientists formerly occupied by World War II suddenly turned their attentions to food production, and the resulting increase caused global populations to soar. During the early 1960s, post-war populations matured and began to want homes, cars, motorbikes, manufactured goods and processed foods. To meet the global demand for goods, manufacturers sought out cheap labour, and cities in developing nations soon became dormitories to their factories. With no Clean Air Acts and governments anxious to provide jobs, factory owners had a free hand to pollute and dump toxic waste. Asian pollution travels westward on prevailing winds in what climatologists call the "Asian Express." When the Asian Express reaches North America it falls in behind American and Canadian pollution headed for Europe, and in Europe the chain is complete when the whole dirty air mass heads for Asia. Ring around the rosy, and while the short term is giving gardeners a pocketful of posies owing to increased carbon dioxide in the atmosphere, the long term could see a repeat of the infamous "Year Without a Summer." In 1815, a volcanic eruption in Sumatra blanketed the Earth with debris that blotted out the sun in the Northern Hemisphere. One result was that there was no summer in 1816. No sun, no fun and millions shivered and starved.

I know, you are thinking pollution causes global warming, not cooling. It does, if the sun's radiation actually reaches the Earth, but if those warming rays reflect back into space before they reach Earth—brrrr.

Global Dimming

The Earth is warming, but at the same time, the amount of sunlight striking it is waning, and many scientists think cleaning up the atmosphere will be akin to throwing a whole pile of logs onto the fire of global warming. Burning fossil fuel causes particulates—tiny bits of carbon soot and ash—to float about in the atmosphere like tiny mirrors that reflect sunlight and keep it from reaching the Earth. They cool us, but at the same time change the composition of clouds. More particulates mean more water droplets in clouds, and water reflects radiation. Can you see the twofold problem? Particulates and the so-called greenhouse gases like carbon dioxide and methane work in tandem; removing particulates would increase the insulating affects of the gases and temperatures would rise dramatically. Inversely, if greenhouse gases alone were removed,

carbon particulates would reflect the sun's rays, and the Earth would freeze. Dirty clouds have actually been masking the true effect of global warming.

Europeans have seen it, because the cleaner they make their air the more greenhouse gas problems they encounter. In 2003, a massive heat wave killed thousands in France and caused massive fires in Portugal and Spain. If you are thinking conundrum, you are right, as we seem damned if we do and damned if we do not. One thing seems obvious; the world must clean up its air and at the same time cut way back on greenhouse gas emissions. The problem is, it takes a long time for gases to leach from the atmosphere, so the removal process of both will be something of a balancing act.

FACTS

A total root length of 620 kilometres has been measured under a single rye plant.

Effects of Climate Change on Gardens

The short-term effects of climate change on Canadian gardens will probably be beneficial—a longer growing season with perhaps two crops possible in some areas owing to increased CO_2 in the atmosphere. The long-term affect is anybody's guess. It may entail changing rainfall patterns, drought and water rationing. Desert conditions may prevail in verdant areas, increasing soil erosion and causing crops to fail. Fresh water is already a valued global commodity and in years to come wars will be fought over diversion of this precious resource.

WATER

We think of the world as a blue, watery marble, but with 97.5% of it seawater and almost 2% locked up

118

in polar ice caps, fresh water is a rare commodity on this planet. However, Canada is blessed with an abundant supply—20% of the world's fresh water is contained within our borders, but only 9% of the drinking stuff is renewable, meaning we have lots of a limited supply.

Canadians use water as if it comes from a bottomless well, and we are second only to Americans in wastage. We use 350 litres a day, while our neighbours to the south go through almost 400; meaningless figures until compared with what the rest of the world uses: 30 litres.

Selling our water has become a contentious issue for both government and private sectors. The federal government fears selling any will turn the stuff into a commodity and subject it to the terms of the General Agreement of Tariffs and Trade (GATT) and the North American Free Trade Act (NAFTA)—rightly so: water is a sacred trust for future generations of Canadians. The problem is, the Americans hold the drain plug for much of that sacred trust and can dredge canals off the Mississippi River at anytime. They have signed agreements not to do so, but when U.S. government administrations change, so do the policies. What can we do about it if they decide to take our water? Nothing, and if we put up a fuss they might just decide to divert some our northward-flowing rivers south.

Freshwater shortage is a already a global problem and it's getting worse; a UN-sponsored study found that by the year 2025, a full 25% of the world's countries will be short of fresh water, and many of their strategists think future wars will be fought over water. There are too many people on this planet and almost all its problems are

symptomatic of overcrowding. Instead of spending trillions of dollars trying to fix the symptoms, governments should be working together to solve the problem of overcrowding.

Readers who know my other books are already aware that I am a big fan of the British theoretical physicist, Freeman Dyson. To quote Dyson,

> I'm not saying global warming doesn't cause problems, obviously it does. I'm saying the problems are being grossly exaggerated. They take away money and attention from other problems that are much more urgent and important. Poverty, infectious diseases, public education and health—not to mention the preservation of living creatures on land and in the oceans.

Dyson is a pragmatist and his advice to gardeners is to make hay while the sun shines. Rising CO_2 levels mean better growing plants and if the levels become too high, we can plant a billion trees and soak it up like a sponge.

FACTS

Canada has 20% of the world's fresh water, but only 9% is a renewable resource.

Around 60% of Canada's fresh water flows north, a tantalizing phenomenon to American states parched for water and looking for new sources.

In Canada's Atlantic provinces, approximately 40% of urban populations are not serviced by sewage-treatment facilities.

Keeping groundwater free of contaminants is important to Canadians—around 26% of the population depends on it for a water supply.

An estimated two million water wells are in Canada, with around 35,000 new wells drilled annually.

It takes 300,000 litres of water to manufacture 900 kilograms of paper, and 86,000 litres of water are needed to produce 900 kilograms of steel.

It takes 1000 litres of water to grow 1 kilogram of potatoes, and 10 litres to manufacture 1 litre of gasoline.

One litre of oil will contaminate 2 million litres of water.

WILD FOODS

Once-popular foods grew wild in our forests, meadows and woodlots, and I think it weird that so many have simply dropped off the gastronomic map. Settlers arriving in Canada during the 18th century could look forward to years of hard work sustained by a diet of bush meat and the ubiquitous lyed corn, or mush. Boiling corn kernels in a lye solution to remove skins and then washing and drying the hearts, or hominy, produces a kind of rough Cream of Wheat, or lyed corn. Settlers brought barrels of the stuff to their new farms, along with the seed to grow more corn. Boiling lyed corn produced gruel, commonly called "mush"—boiled rabbit and mush every night, and on Sundays, baked rabbit and mush. Those settlers had a hard life.

Many pioneer families were lucky—the noise they made cutting trees to clear land attracted the attention of Native peoples who often took pity on the strangers and showed them how to forage wild foods. Can you imagine the settlers' delight when presented with fresh foods, along with a natural pharmacy to cure their ills? All manner of berries grow in Canadian forests: barberries, haw berries, blueberries, chokecherries, wild cherries and grapes, pin cherries, cranberries, salmonberries and a host of others. Settlers learned to harvest wild leeks, carrots and radishes, and if that was not enough, they learned to prepare cattail hearts and milkweed pods, to make tea with spruce tips and flavour foods with wild mustard and sheep sorrel. Mushrooms were gathered and dried in late summer and fall, while spring was set aside for making sugar out of syrup made from the sap of birch and maple trees. One can only imagine the delight of those settlers when they learned how to sweeten their mush simply by boiling sap from trees.

When the 19th century brought new waves of settlers to Canada, the foraging and preparation of wild foods had become pioneer cuisine and favourite recipes were written down and passed about at church socials and community picnics. Trading wild foods with indigenous tribes remained a custom long after the rush for furs had subsided and local general stores across the country carried stocks of birch and maple sugar, wild rice, wild rice flour, mustard and various fruit leathers.

Most people are surprised that fruit leathers were an invention of First Nations tribes—they seem more a modern product of conglomerate candy companies. All First Nations peoples prepared for winter by preserving cooked meat macerated with berries and fat in a leather bag: pemmican. It gave early voyageurs quick, nutritious meals as they plied the length and breadth of the countryside searching out furs.

Dried berries were integral to pemmican, but some berries were saved for fruit leathers. Pounded into long, chewy strips and hung to dry, fruit leathers were kept for the wintertime enjoyment of both adults and children. Nowadays, fruit leathers made from poor-quality fruit bear no resemblance to those our ancestors enjoyed, but the art of making a really good fruit leather is not lost. All across the country, a few people still make and sell quality wild fruit leathers. If you have a hankering to try some, go online and find a supplier. My favourite is Forbes Wild Foods. Mister Forbes has done a lot to preserve Canadian heritage wild foods and he makes them available to the public. He and his small army of foragers deserve our support,

and not trying wild foods is missing out on taste treats that helped make Canada what it is today.

Foraging wild foods is again becoming a popular activity. Many people think that all you need is some time in the forest and a guidebook—a bad idea, because some wild foods have inedible look-a-likes that may cause a trip to the hospital. A good idea is to seek out an expert foraging guide and participate in conducted field trips. You will learn what is available for picking in your area, how to harvest to maintain sustainability and how to prepare what you have foraged. Foragers from every province are online, and some provincial parks feature wild food identification courses. Search around, and you will find someone in your area teaching the ins and outs of shopping wild. In the western provinces, forest guides are an absolute necessity, because stomping about unescorted can get you lost, trespassing or in conflict with another expert forager: the bear.

If you live in BC, plan to attend the annual Shop the Wild Festival, held at Victoria's Royal Roads University during the first days of October. There you can buy foraged or wild crafter products from around 50 vendors, talk shop and get tips on where and when to go and who to go with. Just check the website for information.

Outfitters and lodges in the northern reaches of most provinces sometimes offer edible plant tours and workshops so you can forage for plants the way early fur traders did when they wanted to liven up their meals of pemmican and mush cakes.

There are around a thousand edible wild plants in Canadian forests, and most forests belong to the Crown—the public is free to shop till they drop. West coasters can traipse into the forest and return loaded with wild leeks and berries to make sauces for salmon and Dungeness crab. In central Canada, they forage wild leeks, ginger and mushrooms for roast pork and grilled steaks, and on the east coast, nothing goes better with lobster than fresh picked, newly sprouted fiddleheads.

The Wild Fruit and Nut Store is Open

To identify the following wild edibles, consult a guidebook and make doubly sure you have the correct species of plant before consuming any fruits, nuts or tubers, as some are toxic. The following are but a smattering of wild edibles available to expert foragers, but the ones listed are easily identified and safe to eat.

- STAGHORN AND SMOOTH SUMAC
  Sumacs (*Rhus* spp.) grow all across Canada—the staghorn in the East, the smooth in the West, and where the twains meet, sometimes a hybrid of both is found. The trees are small, and the dense candles of bright red fruit snap off easily like dried twigs. Pick in mid-summer when their flavour is best and either cook as a side dish or juice them for jellies or ades.

APPLE-SUMAC JELLY

$3\frac{1}{2}$ cups sumac juice
  (see instructions)
$2\frac{1}{2}$ cups apple juice
1 cup cranberry juice

Rinse the sumac fruit clusters, cover with water and boil gently for 10 minutes. When cooled, crush through a sieve and strain through a jelly bag. Make apple and cranberry juice the same way and combine the juices in a large pot. Stir in 1 packet of pectin, bring to a boil, add 8 cups of sugar and boil hard for 1 minute. Take off the heat, skim, bottle and seal.

- **WILD SUNFLOWER SEEDS**
Growing in fields and pastures, and alongside river and streams, the wild sunflower (*Helianthus* spp.) is identical to the cultivated variety, except smaller. The cultivated variety will revert to the wild if left unattended, so expect the same number and taste in seeds.

- **OREGON GRAPE**
Oregon grape (*Berberis* spp.) is not really a grape, but a member of the Barberry family. The fruit is round and blue with a touch of waxy white coating. Found only in BC and Alberta, the fruit is juicy and sour. Juice Oregon grapes to make wine or jelly.

- **MAY APPLE**
Another member of the Barberry family, the may apple (*Podophyllum peltatum*) is found mainly in southern Ontario and Quebec in deciduous woods and wet meadowlands. May apple fruit is oval shaped and yellowish green, and is best picked in late summer. Make a juice from the fruit and use it for pie fillings, jellies or ades with a flavour similar to passion fruit.

- **HAZELNUTS (FILBERTS)**
Hazelnuts (*Corylus* spp.) are large shrubs that come in two varieties, one with bristles and the other with a softer nut sheath. Both are found in wooded areas across Canada, and both produce the same delicious nut—albeit a bit smaller than the commercial variety. Crack the kernels open, roast the green nuts in an oven at 180° C, add salt and munch away.

- **ELDERBERRIES**
There are three species of elderberry (*Sambucus* spp.) in Canada, but only two are worth tracking

down, the Canada elder and blue-berried elder. The tiny blue-black, shiny berries form in easily picked clusters and juicing is recommended. Simply simmer the fruit in one-quarter their volume of water for 25 minutes, mash and strain. The juice can be fermented into a palatable wine, mixed with sugar and boiled into jelly, or used to make a superb pancake/waffle syrup.

- HIGH-BUSH CRANBERRY
Of the dozen or so varieties of this member of the Honeysuckle family, only a few have berries worth foraging: the high-bush, squash, nanny, hobblebush and raisin berry. All are delicious berries and range in colour from red to bluish black. High-bush cranberries grow all across southern Canada; squashberry does too, but in areas that are more northern. Hobblebush grows from the east coast to the Great Lakes, nannyberries from Quebec to Manitoba, and wild raisin from Newfoundland to Manitoba.

- WILD BLUEBERRIES, BILBERRIES, HUCKLEBERRIES AND WHORTLEBERRIES
Around 20 species of *Vaccinium* grow in Canada, and depending on the locale, most are called blueberries, or huckleberries. In some areas of the country, even cranberries are called huckleberries. Whatever you call them, they are the most prized and tasty fruits and well worth the forage. Delicious cakes, pies, jellies and syrups await the forager of the plentiful blueberry; so take along an extra pail.

- RED AND BLACK CURRANTS
With 10 species found in Canada, these members (*Ribes* spp.) of the Gooseberry family are not hard to find. Look in moist woodlands and along the banks of streams and rivers. A few species, such

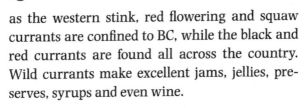

as the western stink, red flowering and squaw currants are confined to BC, while the black and red currants are found all across the country. Wild currants make excellent jams, jellies, preserves, syrups and even wine.

- Gooseberries

Wild gooseberries (also *Ribes* spp.) are found all across the country except in the north. They look and taste like the cultivated variety and are used in the same manner for jam, jellies, preserves and tarts.

- Red Mulberry

Native to Canada, red mulberry trees (*Morus* spp.) grow naturally in the deciduous forests of southern Ontario, but they are used as an ornamental nationwide. Ripe mulberries are delicious and may be eaten off the tree, or baked into pies and cakes. To harvest ripe fruit, spread a cloth under the tree and shake the tree limbs with a pole. Do not eat unripe fruit or touch the milky sap of stems and leaves—both are slightly toxic.

- Saskatoon Berries

There are over a dozen species of saskatoon berry (*Amelanchier* spp.) native to Canada. They can be foraged in every province, but are most abundant in the West. Sweetness of ripe berries varies with species, area and weather conditions, while their abundance can make bears a constant hazard. Sweet, ripe saskatoon berries resemble blueberries in appearance and taste and find use in the same gastronomic manner. A member of the Rose family, the saskatoon berry is packed full of antioxidants and cancer-fighting anthocyanins—good for you, and very tasty.

- CHOKECHERRIES

  Sometimes called wild cherries, chokecherries
  (*Prunus virginiana*) grow across the country and
  are easy to harvest—the cherries grow in clusters.
  Also easy is ascertaining when the fruit is ripe,
  because if not, you will choke. Chokecherries make
  wonderful pies, but you will need patience to
  extract the seeds, so people without patience turn
  them into juice for delicious jellies, syrups and
  ades. Chokecherries are a close relative to the
  black cherry, found mostly in southern Ontario.

- OTHER BERRIES

  Wild strawberries, cloudberries, raspberries, black-
  berries, mountain ash berries and wild grape are
  out there and waiting for you and your pail. Bears
  also adore wild berries, so when foraging in bear
  country, always sing, or take along a radio and
  play it loud.

- BLACK WALNUT AND BUTTERNUT

  Of the 15 or so species of walnuts (*Juglans*) found
  around the world, two are native to Canada—the
  black walnut and butternut, and both are worthy
  of foraging. Pick nuts from the ground in late fall,
  husk and leave them to dry a few months before
  cracking. Black walnuts are superior in flavour to
  the English or American commercial walnut and
  make wonderful toppings for pies, salads and ice
  cream. Butternuts are extremely oily, and a good
  quality oil can be recovered by boiling and skim-
  ming. Butternuts are yummy when roasted, but
  are also great for pickling.

- HICKORY NUTS

  When the first settlers arrived in Quebec and
  Ontario, hickory (*Carya* spp.) was a prominent tree,
  especially shagbark hickory, the tree with the mar-
  vellous nuts and iron-hard wood. Alas, wood won

129

out over nuts, and most trees were turned into axe handles, wagon spokes and chips to smoke pig parts. However, fall foragers in Quebec and Ontario who do run across solitary trees reap a huge reward of delicious treats that need only picking off the ground.

SALTED NUTS

Place 2 cups walnuts or butternuts in a bowl with 1 Tbsp oil, and toss. Sprinkle with 1 or 2 tsp salt, spread evenly on a cookie sheet and bake at 150° C for 10 minutes.

FACTS

Walnut, butternut and hickory all contain a sweet sap tapped by First Nations people along with maple and birch sap; the saps were boiled into sugar or syrup.

Look carefully at the tiny product label on apples and other fruits. A four-digit number indicates the fruit has been grown in a conventional manner; a five-digit number beginning with "9" indicates organically grown fruit, while five digits beginning with "8" indicate a genetically modified fruit.

Those supermarket apple pies you think are baked in-store are probably made in Kentville, Nova Scotia, by Sarsfield Foods, a Weston company. Sarsfield use over 15 million pounds of Northern Spy apples to bake an incredible 10 million pies annually.

WEIRD HORTICULTURAL HAPPENINGS

In 2008, Canada had its usual ration of crop circles (we average about five annually), a fisherman in PEI caught a bright yellow lobster, Jake Van Kooten of Port Alberni, BC, grew a 696.95 kilogram pumpkin, and researchers in Ontario found another 1000 perfectly round forest rings.

Scientists study crop circles but have never come to a unanimous conclusion as to their authenticity. The yellow lobster is a 1 in 300 million fluke of nature. Jake Van Kooten's pumpkin turned out to be a world record, while the forest rings, attributed to everything from electrometric pulses to leaking methane gas, are still a mystery.

In the spring of 2009, blue jays and robins appeared in Pangnirtung, Nunavut, for the first time in recorded history, and a quarter of Canada's honeybees disappeared for the third year in a row. The birds must have given Baffin Island residents a treat, but the vanishing bees have scientists very worried. They call it Colony Collapse Disorder, or CCD, and it is affecting bee populations worldwide.

- CROP CIRCLES
  They appear all over the world and have been doing so for centuries; around 800 AD, the Bishop of Lyon wrote to a priest about to take over a new parish near Lyon, warning him of devil worship by some of his new parishioners. The bishop explained in his letter that devil worshippers were taking seeds out of flattened crop circles and

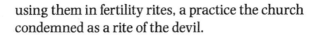

using them in fertility rites, a practice the church condemned as a rite of the devil.

The earliest picture of a crop circle appears in a 1678 woodcut entitled "Strange News out of Hartford-shire." It depicts a devil cutting a pattern into a grain field with a scythe. The text with the image tells of a farmer refusing to pay a labourer for cutting oats, and quotes him as saying, "I would rather have the devil cut my oats." According to the text, the farmer awoke the next morning to find his entire crop cut into a series of exact circles; the text notes that the farmer was so afraid he dared not set foot into the field.

Circles that may or may not be crop related are in prehistoric wall carvings and ancient pictographs and on Egyptian tombs. Crop circles have a long history, but until the beginning of the 20th century, the scientific community considered every one an elaborate hoax. Many crop circles are indeed hoaxes, so researchers have established requirements as to what constitutes a circle worth investigation:

- Elongated apical plant stem nodes
- Expulsion cavities in the plant stem nodes
- The presence of 10 to 50 micrometer-sized magnetized spheres distributed evenly in the soil
- No sign of human presence, influence or tool marks.

Crop circles have appeared in 28 countries around the globe. England has recorded the most and largest circles. In 2001, a circle found in an English field had a diameter of 274 metres and contained a pattern of 409 smaller circles. Since the 1930s, more than 10,000 crop circles have been reported worldwide, while 250 new ones are reported every year, yet nobody has ever witnessed the construction of a circle. They somehow just appear, sometimes accompanied by a bright light, with most stumbled upon by the farmer or property owner.

In England, two men admitted to creating hundreds of circles, but many experts doubt their story because the time required for constructing so many lay beyond their capabilities and because someone would have surely would have spotted their midnight artistry. Noted cereologist Colin Andrews believes that around 80% of crop circles are hoaxes perpetrated by humans, but the other 20% he attributes to unknown forces.

In western Canada, other types of grain anomalies occur on a regular basis and seem somehow related to crop circles. Lodged grain, while not falling in circles, does have repeated internal patterns and node damage similar to crop circles. While many people claim weather is responsible for lodged grain designs, examination of the fields reveals no evidence of wind or hail damage. Lodged grain stalks break at the top node, as do crop circle grain stalks, and fall one way, while the stalk falls at a right angle with the grain heads falling in another direction.

Many people believe crop circles have a connection with UFOs—although no one has witnessed the construction of a crop circle, plenty of witnesses have noted weird lights in the vicinity of found circles. Some people claim their infirmities are cured or symptoms relieved by walking into crop circles. Increased nitric oxide levels are found in most circles; nitric oxide is a naturally occurring chemical in human bodies that aids in

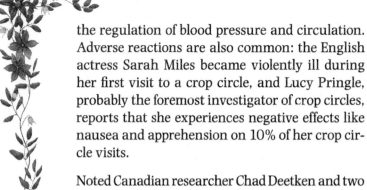

the regulation of blood pressure and circulation. Adverse reactions are also common: the English actress Sarah Miles became violently ill during her first visit to a crop circle, and Lucy Pringle, probably the foremost investigator of crop circles, reports that she experiences negative effects like nausea and apprehension on 10% of her crop circle visits.

Noted Canadian researcher Chad Deetken and two associates entered a crop circle in Saskatchewan called the Watmough formation, and each lay down in a separate section to test whether they would experience anything out of the ordinary. "Out of the ordinary" happened to each at exactly the same moment: Chad Deetken endured muscle tension and difficulty breathing, while his companions, hearing footsteps and thinking they were about to be stepped upon by something large, ran from the circle. Hearing phantom footsteps in circles is reported often, as are hearing clicking noises. People who have consumed grain taken from crop circles report an increase in energy comparable to taking amphetamines.

The formation of crop circles has no destructive effect on grain stalks other than cavities in the stem nodes, but a person would not want to be in on a formation. On August 21, 1992, farmer Joe Rennik of Milestone, Saskatchewan, discovered several lodged rectangular grain formations in his wheat field. It looked like a stone had skipped across the field. Intrigued, he walked through the formations and found a large, completely flat porcupine; legs splayed, the large animal had been flattened to a thickness of only 3". Exploded birds have been reported at various English circles; in some cases, whole flocks have simply disintegrated, covering every felled grain stalk with blood.

- FOREST RINGS

On the ground, you can walk straight through a forest circle and notice nothing unusual, but from the air, they stand out like warts on a baby's bum. Forest rings come in all sizes, from 30 metres wide to several kilometres, but in only one shape: perfect circles. How many there are is a guess, but estimates put the number at 7000 to 8000. They are found all over Canada and are not confined to forests—many are in farmers' fields. Unlike crop circles, forest circles are indelibly marked into the earth. What they are and how they came to be are ongoing mysteries. Some scientists claim they are old meteor craters, and others say the cause is electrochemical cells of negatively charged energy produced by metal or methane gas deposits. Most scientists will simply shrug their shoulders.

Perhaps the rings are forest-eating fungi, similar to the giant discovered in Oregon. Smaller versions of fungi rings, called fairy rings, are a perpetual curse to golf course groundskeepers, as their appearance means an invasion of the dreaded grass snatcher (*Maramius oreades*), a mushroom species that delights eating in the round.

Whatever the cause, northern Ontario plays host to most of the planet's mysterious forest rings, with some found in southern Ontario, Quebec, the Yukon, Australia and Russia.

- DISAPPEARING BEES

The beekeeper is like any other business operator; he or she worries about the workers, the high cost of supplies and the price of goods produced. However, very few business operators wake up in the morning to find their factory workers have flown the coop. The office manager (queen bee) is still in

the factory, as are all the young trainees (immature workers) but not one worker remains, and there are no dead ones around the hive.

This weird disappearance of worker bees, called Colony Collapse Disorder or CCD, is affecting hives around the world. One day the hive is full of busy workers gathering and storing honey, and the next day they are gone. CCD is causing great angst for scientists who cannot put a finger on the cause. Some claim it is a natural cycle, others blame insecticides, electromagnetic energy, virus, fungus or a combination.

One thing they do agree on is how much trouble the world will be in if they cannot find the cause—roughly 40% of global crop production depends on honeybees for pollination. European scientists are even warning of a complete demise of the honeybee and blame neonicotinoid insecticides. Those same scientists also claim that CCD is an invented disease sold to the public by the giant pharmaceutical companies to direct attention from their bee-killing insecticides. German and French governments have agreed with those scientists and banned neonicotinoid insecticides, the Germans for all crops, the French for sunflowers and corn seed.

Neonicotinoids are systemic insecticides similar to nicotine and applied by treating both commercial and garden seeds. The chemical has been hugely successful in controlling chewing and sucking insects and is used extensively on North American food crops. In Canada, corn, canola and potato seeds are treated with neonicotinoid insecticides.

Spanish scientists claim a parasitic fungus called *Nosema ceranae* is responsible for CCD, and that a dose of the antibiotic will solve the problem. Israeli scientists say a virus is responsible, while those in India claim it is a bee mite called *Varroa destructor.*

Whatever the cause, and excuse my rant, the world is in danger of losing the backbone of global food production. If that should occur quickly, worldwide economic melt down will surely follow. How can we allow that to happen? Canadian and U.S. legislators recently spent billions of tax dollars bailing out banks and companies that deserved bankruptcy, and what are they spending to save the bees, a few million dollars? Has either government stopped the sale of neonicotinoid insecticides? No, because neither government wants to take on the combined might of pharmaceuticals, potatoes and corn.

Not upsetting apple carts is standard government policy, but if those bees keep disappearing, heads will eventually roll—but only figuratively, and that will be a shame. Honeybees are one of the Creator's great gifts to mankind, and to treat them in such a despicable manner for profit is such an effrontery that doing without seems fit punishment. If the honeybee goes, the world learns to do without half its food, while we gardeners will have to learn to pollinate with a brush and make do without honey.

FAMOUS GARDENS YOU MUST SEE ON YOUR TRAVELS
- The Humble Administrator's Garden in Suzhou, China, and the Imperial Summer Palace in Beijing
- The Boboli Gardens in Florence, Italy, and the Vatican Gardens
- The Adachi Museum Garden in Shimane, Japan

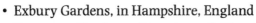

- Exbury Gardens, in Hampshire, England
- Eyrignac, Hambury Botanic and Versailles gardens in France
- The Hawaii Tropical Botanical Gardens north of Hilo on the Big Island of Hawaii
- The Royal Botanical Gardens in Burlington, Ontario
- Huntington Botanical Gardens, the Japanese Friendship Garden and Central Park in New York
- The National Botanic Gardens and Belair National Park in Australia
- The famous Schoenbrunn Palace Gardens in Vienna, Austria
- Germany has many gardens, but the Botanical Garden of Justus-Liebig University in Giessen is most famous
- The Alhambra in Granada, Spain
- Best for last is the Keukenhof Gardens in Lisse, Netherlands.

ORGANIC FOODS

Produce from your garden is, or should be, of a quality commonly referred to as "organic"—no pesticides, no herbicides, no synthetic fertilizers and no long days stacked in a truck. Just fresh, wholesome greens that taste good and are good for you, the way food used to be. You might wonder how our nation's food supply got so off track that it needs a special designation for consumers to identify "real" from "pseudo" food. The truth is, it never got off track, it simply took a different direction and moved away from small towns and farming communities.

When World War II broke out, Canadians not in the services did their bit in city-based armament factories. After the war, many workers and returning servicemen decided to stay in the cities and raise families. They needed housing, and both the federal government and the construction industry pitched in to build assembly-line homes on the outskirts of cities in subdivisions. None of the planners and architects of these subdivisions gave a thought to a food supply. Small-town Canada got its fresh seasonal vegetables from local farmers' markets and its canned goods and root vegetables from corner stores. However, in the "burbs," there were no farmers' markets and population densities were too low to support corner stores. Outside of milk delivery, stocking the household pantry meant a long, once-a-week shopping trip into the city. Milk was important to families and dairies had a moral obligation to deliver no matter where people chose to live. Up until the 1960s, home-building codes across Canada included a mandatory, built-in dairy

box for the milkman to deposit his wares. Dairies saw opportunity in the burbs and loaded their milk trucks with staples such as eggs, butter and bread to stuff the milk boxes. Alas, it was not enough to put off the dreaded once-a-week shopping trip and the vehicles of suburbanites would pack the roads every Saturday.

FACTS

The crab apple is a native Canadian fruit tree. Pioneer women used the fruit in jelly and jam making, and gristmill operators used its hard wood to make gears and water blades for their mills.

Until 1945, most Canadian apples shipped to overseas markets went packed in wooden barrels.

The organic crop most grown in Canada may surprise you—it is hay. Canada is geographically perfect for growing hay: wide expanses of prairie allow for intensive mechanized planting and harvesting. We grow and export a lot of hay to the United States for use in their organic dairy operations. American goats and dairy cows like our hay, and their owners are willing to pay a premium for the product.

"Premium" is a key word in organic agriculture; organically produced food tastes better, is better for you and does not spoil as quickly. The rub is that it costs more to produce, and the food business is extremely cost conscious. Think of it as being an auction, which is what agribusiness was in the beginning. Food manufacturers and retailers both wanted the most for the least amount of money—as do the consumers—and they are unwilling to pay a premium. Will organic foods ever achieve mainstream acceptance by consumers already balking at paying high prices for commercially produced foods? That remains to be seen, but it is doubtful supermarkets will offer more than token samples of organically grown foods. Without supermarkets, organic growers are confined to supplying small, specialized shops and selling in local farmers' markets.

Another rub is global overpopulation: is it fair for starvation to occur in some countries while Canada entertains organic food production? Is this situation not a glaring example of the rich getting richer and the poor getting poorer, or how not to win friends and influence people? On the other hand, if developing countries allow unfettered population growth, why should Canada shoulder the responsibility of making up for shortfalls when their food becomes scarce owing to weather and plant disease?

That will have to be the political mindset if Canadians decide they want their foods organically grown, as crop yields will decrease drastically along with surpluses available to fight hunger in have-not countries. Ironically, most of the agricultural output from these have-not countries is grown organically and in quantities sufficient to feed their populations if not for their out-of-control birthrates.

When Napoleon Bonaparte invaded Egypt in 1798, the population was around three million, and every citizen subsisted on organically grown foods. In a little more than two centuries, the population of Egypt has surpassed 83 million, almost half that figure coming in the last 40 years owing to increased agricultural productivity made possible by the infamous green revolution. Modern Egypt depends on fertilizers, huge irrigation projects and gene-modified crops with questionable resistance to disease. With 90% of the country's ever-expanding population concentrated in cities along the Nile and the Suez delta, there is no margin for agricultural misadventure. If their crops fail, 83 million people will not be looking east to Mecca for help, they will be looking west.

Even without crop failure, the expected rise in sea levels from global warming will inundate Egypt's agricultural lands and cause mass starvation. You would think that with these problems hanging over their heads, the Egyptian government would act to reverse overpopulation. Egypt is just one of many countries doing nothing to combat overpopulation, and Canadians must therefore think long and hard about the national trend towards organic foods. Do we eat healthier, with less to share, or do we let whole nations reap the folly of their ways and starve?

As of 2009, Canadian consumers have a new logo on organically grown, packaged food products. Canada has finally instituted a national standard for organic agriculture, and the logo guarantees consumers that at least 95% of the product in the package contains organically grown ingredients. It also guarantees that nothing in the package is produced from genetically engineered seed, no sewage sludge was used as soil amendment, no synthetic growth regulators, no fertilizers that contain prohibited substances, no gamma rays used in preservation, and only natural insecticides have been used on the product. The government has borrowed the American set of standards, and both are interchangeable since around 80% of organic food consumed in Canada comes from the U.S.

FACTS

Natural insecticides from plant sources are a permitted adjunct for organic crops. The common organic insecticides permitted are *Bacillus thuringiensis* (*Bt*), pyrethrum, derived from chrysanthemum flowers, and rotenone, derived from the roots of several species of tropical plants. Rotenone is toxic to freshwater snails and some fish species, and causes Parkinson's disease when injected into rats.

A 2007 European Union study found organically grown fruits and vegetables contained 40% more antioxidants than equivalent conventional grown foods. Organic milk was even more of a surprise—it contained 60% more antioxidants.

The American organic food industry has another logo initiative under way, the Non-GMO (genetically modified organism) identity program. GMOs can be found in most food products consumed around the world, especially in North America. To counter this trend, an organics industry group is promoting the Non-GMO seal as a way of assuring customers that every precaution has been taken to keep member products free of genetically modified ingredients. The seal, a butterfly perched on two blades of grass, made its appearance on American-made organic food products during the fall of 2009, at about the same time the North American sugar beet industry began using GMO seed. In 2010, half the sugar produced in America will come from gene-engineered plants, while in Canada, Rogers Sugar/Lantic is already growing and processing beet sugar from GMO crops and plans to expand its program to include cane sugar.

Redpath, another large Canadian sugar producer, uses only cane sugar free of GMOs—the choice is yours, but there is a fly in the ointment, as the wind may soon remove any consumer choices. As wind carries pollen from one field to another, all food crops including wheat will soon be genetically contaminated, a situation that seems destined to derail the organic food business.

Food like Grandma made will soon be just a memory, and the whole of Canada will have to hold its breath and await the long-term effects, if any, of consuming genetically altered foods.

Gardeners will not be among those breath holders, but only if they make sure their seeds are GMO free and from reputable dealers. Don't gamble with the health of you and yours; just plant a vegetable garden.

FACTS

Conventional farmers have an arsenal of around 300 different insecticides to use on foods destined for the shelves of supermarkets.

Food processors have an arsenal of around 500 ingredients to beef up foods destined for the shelves of supermarkets.

Food producers can display the organic designation logo if ingredients are grown on land previously farmed by conventional means but allowed to lay fallow for several years. Unfortunately, certain trace minerals such as magnesium, copper, cobalt, manganese and iron may have been exhausted from the land and will take years to be replaced by natural methods.

WEIRD PLANTS

Large, isolated islands allow for millions of years of protected species evolution and are home to some of the weirdest flora on the planet. Madagascar, an isolated island in the Indian Ocean, supports no less than six of the world's nine species of succulent baobab (*Adansonia* spp.) trees. Baobabs are caudiciform plants, which means that they store water in a caudex, a swollen trunk, and some caudexes are out-of-this-world weird. Sometimes called "upside-down trees" because their branches remind us of tree roots, baobabs grow slowly, with some island trees clocking in at over 1600 years. Much older trees probably existed, but overpopulation is ravaging the forests of Madagascar, and large trees are disappearing at an alarming rate. Baobabs come in all sizes—tall with slender trunks, short with fat trunks and some have trunks you have to see to believe.

Succulent trees grow all over Madagascar. *Pachypodium lameri*, or Madagascar palm, grows in the south and

---

Garden Joke
Thanks to Martha's garden, she and husband Sam lived long and fruitful lives until the day she ran the car into a telephone pole, killing them both. Ka-bang, and when they opened their eyes, there was paradise: blue sky, flowers everywhere, a bubbling brook, and tiny angels to fulfill their every desire. Still a bit miffed over the pole-slamming incident, Sam turned to Martha, and said, "Silly woman, if it not for you and your garden, we could have been here years ago."

looks more palm tree than the chubby baobabs, while another, *Moringa oleifera*, looks similar to the baobab but has leaves like a willow tree. *Pachypodium rosulatum*, or elephant's feet, have round trunks and would be mistaken for boulders without their stubby branches. Baobab trees are sold as novelty plants worldwide and almost everyone recognizes them, but to see them in the wild in such diversity and size is an experience not to be missed. Single species grow in other countries, but in Madagascar, six are on parade and make for an unforgettable sight. An interesting aside is the way two of Madagascar's six baobab species encourage pollination; they produce large flowers to attract bats and lemurs.

Another set of succulents that issued from Madagascar as novelty plants is the *Kalanchoe* genus, which consists of around 125 species that range in size a from few inches to large trees. The novelty plants sold around the world are the smaller species and so common they are used as garden annuals, but to see a wild kalanchoe tree will stop you in your tracks and have you thinking of *Alice in Wonderland* and the "make me big make me small" scene. Much of Madagascar's flora diversity can be found in retail plant nurseries in a miniaturized form, but to see the grandiose versions in the wild is a memorable experience worth catching before it succumbs to overpopulation and invasive species like the omnipresent Australian eucalyptus trees. Treat yourself and go see the baobabs, the fabled traveller and exploding palms, the spiny forests and the cancer-fighting miracle, the rosy periwinkle, while there is still opportunity.

However, you do not have to travel to the ends of the earth to see island evolution. We have some fantastic examples right here in Canada. Our nation is like a vast arboreal sea that runs uninterrupted for 5514 kilometres, and like all seas, there are small enclaves of evolutionary surprises: islands in the green.

While not as startling in appearance as a baobab or kalanchoe, some of these evolutionary enclaves feature some stunning arboreal inhabitants.

Vancouver Island has the Carmanah Valley with its old-growth forest of giant Sitka spruce, some of which loom an astounding 95 metres tall. On Vancouver Island and nearby areas are the majestic, heaven-touching Douglas-fir trees. These trees must be the Creator's favourite living things, and walking among them is to know there is a heaven. British Columbia also has the Great Bear coastal rainforest, with trees that were tall before Confederation. Here are 2 million hectares of 1000-year-old cedars and 24 other species of trees along with what is probably the greatest diversity of fungi and lichen on the planet. Paradise, and when you see it you will understand about heaven.

Fly northeast into the near arctic of the Northwest Territories, and you will come across the South Nahanni River with its deep gorges and magnificent wildness. A national park within the Mackenzie Mountain system, the South Nahanni features a waterfall twice as high as Niagara (Virginia Falls) and an extensive labyrinth of caves (the valley remained unglaciated during the ice age). Here are fantastic canyons, unique geological formations, hot springs and flora trapped in an evolutionary island. The Nahanni aster (*Aster nahanniesis*) grows here and nowhere else on the planet. Over 700 species of plants have already been identified and new ones are added to the list annually. Orchids grow here, fields of them and within a stone's throw of the Arctic. You can experience the Arctic by travelling a few kilometres north of the Nahanni into a land of tundra and areas with no vegetation. Dry as a desert, but when your aircraft turns, there is the wet and wild Nahanni, an island paradise.

Water is no problem on the islands of Borneo and Sumatra—rain, rain and more rain make for very large and happy plants. One plant, *Rafflesia arnoldii*, commonly called "corpse flower," is one of a genus of 16 known species. It produces the world's largest bloom and is always in the botanical spotlight somewhere. *Rafflesias* are parasitic carrion plants that produce no stems, roots, leaves or chlorophyll for photosynthesis. *R. arnoldii* depends solely on the tissues of *Tetrastigma* vine plants to survive and flower. When it does flower, it bursts through the bark of the vine and sits on the forest floor like a king on a throne. The flower can be 1 metre across, weigh more than 5 kilograms and hold more than 4 litres of nectar to attract flies for pollination. The corpse flower plant was discovered and named by Sir Stanford Raffles and his companion Dr. Joseph Arnold, both probably hesitant at having their names attached to such a vile-smelling species.

Flower size aside, another "carrion plant" makes *R. arnoldii* look puny. It is titan arum (*Amorphophallus titanium*, Greek words for "giant misshapen penis"). The plant's flower (actually an unbranched cluster of flowers) can attain a height of almost 3 metres and have a circumference of more than 2 metres. What's more, the flower tip of titan arum (the "penis") generates body temperature heat that accentuates its peculiar and revolting perfume. London's Kew Gardens and a host of other botanical gardens have titan arums, and all look forward to its flowering with some trepidation—the stink is reminiscent of a rotting elephant carcass. You have to smell to believe, and people want so much to believe that they line up for blocks to get a look and a whiff. Interesting to note, unlike *Rafflesias*, titan arum is not parasitic. Instead, it employs a giant compound leaf resembling a tree for photosynthesis and stores energy in a tuber that may weigh more than 90 kilograms.

Canada has its own corpse flower plant. The ghost flower (*aka* fitroot or Indian pipe; *Monotropa uniflora*) is a member of the wintergreen family. The plant is a saprophyte, meaning it has no chlorophyll and gets nourishment from fungus that grows on rotting vegetation. This pale, sometimes pinkish plant issues a single white flower that resembles a pipe, hence the common name Indian pipe. During the 19th century, juice of the ghost flower saw use by pioneers as eyewash and as a cure for mental problems. Ghost plants look and behave like mushrooms, but they are actually related to laurels, azaleas and rhododendrons. They are true plants, found all over North America, usually under oak and pine trees.

Facts

Once covered in lush forest, the Tenere region of northeastern Nigeria fell victim to desertification in the early 20th century. However, the once-great forest had a survivor, a lone acacia tree that locals considered a challenge from God. The tree became a lighthouse on the Tenere, the last object seen when crossing the great desert, the first when returning. In 1973, the Tenere region's sacred tree was obliterated by a drunken Libyan truck driver and has been replaced by a metal sculpture.

Pineapples are berries, peanuts are beans and avocados have the highest caloric content of any fruit, 167 calories per 100 grams.

Stinkers aside, Borneo and Sumatra abound in parasitic flora; probably the weirdest are the carnivorous plants, the *Nepenthes*, or tropical pitcher plants. Of the 100 or more species of that genus growing worldwide, around 30 are found on the island of Borneo. They come in all colours and some are so large they sometimes catch small animals and lizards. Land crabs like to forage in the plant's caldera, and certain frogs go from eggs to tadpoles to adults completely with the confines of the plant's slippery aquarium. During the latter part of the 19th century, a kind of *Nepenthes* mania consumed the botanical world, and vast collections of the plants were assembled both in public and private conservatories—not surprising, since the plants are engineering marvels and to watch them in action is fascinating. The writer Howard Ashman must have been observing at least one when he wrote his *Nepenthes*-themed musical play, *Little Shop of Horrors*.

As well as having a corpse flower, Canada's islands of evolution also contain carnivorous plants, most notably the pitcher plant, a relative of the tropical *Nepenthes*. Pitcher plants (*Sarracenia*) are native to the North American east coast and include eight species, one of which, *S. purpurea*, is the provincial flower of Newfoundland and Labrador. The plants' prey-catching mechanisms, the pitfall trap, are adapted, rolled leaves that contain glands that secrete honeydew to attract insects and enzymes to break down tissue. Since the pitcher plant does not depend on soil for nutrients, it can inhabit areas other plants avoid, such as high acidic soils or water-saturated bogs.

FACTS

From the late 19th century to the late 1920s, almost all Canadian railway stations featured a lovely garden for passengers to enjoy while awaiting trains. With the rising popularity of automobiles, the railway bosses decided to pave over the gardens to provide parking.

The standard issue of annual seeds to CPR stationmasters for the gardens included alyssum, cornflower, clarkia, scarlet flax, Shirley poppy, California poppy, nasturtium and zinnias.

Weird Plant Tour

- THE MONKEY PUZZLE TREE (*ARAUCARIA ARAUCANA*), BUTCHART GARDENS, VICTORIA, BC
  The monkey puzzle tree is native to the Andes Mountains of South America. Looking like a giant bottlebrush, this weird evergreen thrives at Butchart Gardens and in various locations on Vancouver Island and in Metro Vancouver. In the wild, it may reach heights in excess of 45 metres and live 1000 years. Seeds from its 5 kilogram cones are very tasty and one reason how the tree wound up in 18th-century European botanical collections with a strange name. A touring Scot named Archibald Menzies saw the tree and commented that it would puzzle a monkey to climb to the top. Later over dinner, he tasted some seeds from the tree and stuck a few in his pocket to snack on. Then he forgot about them. Onboard ship and halfway to Europe, Archibald Menzies found his snack seeds and was amazed to see they had germinated.

- GIANT DOUGLAS FIR (*PSEUDOTSUGA MENZIESII*), CATHEDRAL GROVE, MACMILLAN PROVINCIAL PARK, VANCOUVER ISLAND, BC
  Awe inspiring, and if your faith in the Creator is wavering, come here and have it renewed.

- HIMALAYAN BLUE POPPY (*MECONOPSIS BETONICIFOLIA*), GRAND-MÉTIS, QUEBEC, OR UNIVERSITY OF BRITISH COLUMBIA BOTANIC GARDEN, VANCOUVER, BC
An amazing sight, so blue and wondrous a flower you will immediately want some for your garden. Alas, they are almost impossible to grow.

- GINKGO BILOBA (*GINKGO BILOBA*), AN ORNAMENTAL TREE FOUND IN ALMOST EVERY CANADIAN PROVINCE
Thought extinct, this Permian-era tree predates the dinosaurs and was discovered growing in Japan and eastern China. Brought to Europe in the 17th century, the trees were propagated by cuttings and widely used by gardeners as ornamentals. Ginkgos are dioecious, meaning that some trees are male and others female. Males produce cones and females ovules. The ginkgo is unusual in that pollination is by motile sperm, meaning that they can swim to their destination as long as water is present; except for cycads, ferns and lower plants such as mosses and algae, all other plants alive today have nonmotile sperm, which require external forces to propel them onward. Fertilized cells form embryos that develop into seeds containing butyric acid, a chemical that smells like poop. Once formed, the seeds drop off the tree and can really stink up the neighbourhood. Owners of young trees need not worry, however, because it takes about 50 years before a ginkgo flowers.

FACTS

Ginkgo trees growing in Canada are mostly male clones called "Autumn Gold," produced to avoid the stinky seeds.

The Wood's cycad (*Encephalartos woodii*) is a tasty plant consumed almost to extinction. Fermented and ground, the pithy trunks of cycads were used as a source of starch in the diet of the local people. The only specimens ever found by science were a single clump of four males discovered in South Africa's KwaZulu-Natal province in 1895. The species is no longer found in the wild, but offshoots derived from this clump now grow in many botanical gardens around the world. Because only male plants have survived, scientists are using bioengineering in the hope of one day creating a female version of this ancient plant.

Aciphylla horrida, a ferocious-looking member of the carrot family native to New Zealand, is covered with sharp, sword-shaped leaves to defend against...nothing. The plant evolved its defensive mechanism to protect against browsing moas, very large birds that became extinct around 1500 AD.

OUR DISAPPEARING SOIL

All flesh is grass.

—Isaiah 40:6

The Old Testament quotation above is a great line of biblical prose written to illustrate the transitory nature of life. Born, live, die, and the earth will turn you into grass—deep stuff, both the philosophical and the stuff that eats you up: soil.

Gardeners think about soil constantly, but most other people never give it a thought. Homeowners poison it with herbicides; construction companies move it; road, house and railway builders dump it into ravines; mining companies scrape it; and large-scale farming interests over-fertilize and assault it with chemicals.

Civilization has assaulted a lot of soil: 15 million square kilometres ploughed up for farmland, 10 million square kilometres of forest cut down and 32 million square kilometres for livestock grazing. That only leaves 90 million square kilometres, and loggers are attacking that vigorously. Deforestation is progressing so rapidly that just to keep pace with loss and allow for slow regeneration, 250 million trees would have to be planted every year—and we should be doing that because trees use carbon dioxide and modify temperature extremes. Trees also keep soil from eroding, and we need that too, because every year around 75 million tons of precious topsoil is swept away by winds or eroded by rainwater. In 1776, the average depth of topsoil on

U.S. and Canadian prairie lands was 22 centimetres, a mean depth that over the years has diminished to less than 15 centimetres. That's not good, and it gets worse in some undeveloped countries with unfettered population growth, where soil depth is half what it was a century ago. A grim future may await those nations when some time down the road their growing populations may experience starvation on a massive scale.

What is Soil?

Soil is rock material eroded by wind, water and glaciations into grains of various-sized sand: very fine, fine, medium, coarse and very coarse. Clay is rock chemically weathered by weak concentrations of carbonic or other acids leached from upper layers as in the formation of limestone caves. Silt, sometimes called rock flour, is superfine sand usually formed through glaciations. These mineral specks, sand, clay and silt make up about 45% of soil, 50% is water and air, and 5% is organic matter. As all gardeners know, it is a far from perfect formula and needs to be tweaked constantly.

Canadians are lucky, because in large sections of the country the soil comes already tweaked by nature. It is home to all kinds of tiny creatures: bacteria, nematodes, rotifers, fungi, worms, etc.—lots and lots of tiny creatures and all of them are hungry. Lumped together, they work like a stomach: macerating, digesting and creating byproducts of organic matter. Left undisturbed, these microscopic creatures will produce the perfect soil aggregate, the right combination of minerals, water, air and organic matter necessary for stabilization. Without stabilization, soil is at the mercy of weather and will break down and go with the flow, be it wind or rain.

Canada had soil stabilization in many areas, most notably in the great prairies, an endless sea of perennial grasses with deep root structures necessary for over-wintering, aerating soil and contributing organic matter to aggregation. All this changed in the 18th century when settlers arrived to till the land and grow annual crops. These farmers knew nothing of crop rotation and resting the soil. Tilling and planting the same fields shrinks the aggregate size of the soil. The historical record shows that a major drought can be expected every 20 years on the prairies. In the 1920s and 30s, disaster occurred and many Canadian farmers were forced to abandon their land.

Modern farmers avoid using the plough on fields in order to save the soil aggregate and conserve water. Nowadays, any field you see worked over by a tractor is probably only having stubble chopped with a grain harrow after harvest. Today's farmer knows that to hang onto precious soil he or she must protect it from wind and water by not disturbing the organic mat left by the previous crop. So as not to disturb the organic mat, modern farmers plant seed with non-intrusive air guns and reap huge benefits in saved labour and bushel per acre returns.

As well as proper aggregate, most plants need the assistance of a species of soil fungus called "mycorrhiza" to prosper. Different species helping each other is called "a symbiotic relationship" and the plant/mycorrhiza fungi help-fest has been going on for around 500 million years. Plants provide the fungus with carbohydrate sugars produced through photosynthesis and sent from leaves to roots, while the fungus provides plants the use of its mycelium or vegetative part for increased root surface area and better nutrient and water absorption.

Adding mycorrhiza inoculate to both vegetable and flower gardens will see a marked increase in size, quality and yield, and will put a big smile on the face of gardeners. If you cannot find the product at local plant nurseries, order it online.

FACTS

A fungus mycelium found in eastern Oregon is perhaps the largest organism on the planet. Larger than 1600 football fields and estimated to be more than 2000 years old, the Oregon fungus is a forest feeder that has killed and consumed the forest growing above it several times, each time deepening the soil and allowing for the growth of ever-larger trees.

One large portabella (or portobello) mushroom contains more potassium than a banana.

Of the more than 2000 species of mushrooms consumed around the world, the ubiquitous white button mushroom is the most commonly cultivated.

North America loses over 3 billion tons of topsoil annually, with over one-third of the loss attributed to agriculture. The soil is ploughed up, and the wind picks up small bits of it and carries it to who knows where—the ocean, or Africa even, as that continent's soil often winds up in North America. It might be a satisfactory arrangement if what we received in exchange was a soil quality conducive to agriculture and not desert sand. While the wind carries away small bits, it also affects larger soil particles by bouncing them along the ground; this process is called "saltation." In a slow process called "surface creep," ongoing bombardment by saltating particles can move still heavier grains.

Wind erosion is a constant process and can be either speeded up or slowed down by agricultural practices.

If allowed to speed up by overworking the land, fertility can become so compromised the land becomes unsuitable for crops and must remain fallow for decades to regain fertility. After the Great Dustbowl of the 1930s, huge tracts of abandoned farmland became prairie grassland and a place for the buffalo to roam. Some of that land has become fertile again and could soon be raising sugar beets, while the roaming buffalo become burger patties. There can be no hope for man or beast when dirt is turned into dollars, but a few places on the planet have soils worth their weight in gold. Called "loess," it is a wind-borne soil deposit comprising bits of quartz, feldspars, carbonates, clays and a host of other minerals. To have loess in your Back Forty is akin to winning a lottery, as no soil is more fertile or deep.

Loess (pronounced lew-es) is the desert before it became desert, the topsoil sans organic matter. In some areas of China, loess deposits blown in from northern deserts are hundreds of metres thick and form huge bluffs and cliff structures. In Canada, loess is created by glaciations and is broadcast thinly over wide areas; but in some arid sections of Alberta, Saskatchewan and Manitoba loess deposits form huge, dramatic sand dunes. South of our Prairie Provinces, the Great Plains of America owe their fantastic fertility to widespread, wind-borne loess deposits of rock flour created by glacial ice sheets. However, exposed to wind or rain and unprotected by groundcover, Great Plains loess deposits display a marked tendency towards flight, as evidenced by the 1930s dustbowl.

If farmers neglect the land, soil will take to the air and will sometimes leave behind strange landscapes called badlands. Badlands can be found in various places in Canada. One of the largest is the Canadian Badlands, at 9000 square kilometres. It is a place of desolation, fantastic geological formations and dinosaur bones—the area includes Dinosaur Provincial Park, near Drumheller, Alberta.

The badlands in Alberta owe their formation to glacier gouging and erosion, but in Ontario, there is a badlands created entirely by the hand of man. The Cheltenham Badlands is an hour's drive north of Toronto, but it may as well be on the red planet Mars. Red mounds, greenish gullies, shades of grey and the odd stunted tree make the Cheltenham Badlands one of Ontario's weirdest places. The paint-box red of the Cheltenham Badlands is iron oxide scraped from rock by glaciers and deposited onto the floor of a great prehistoric sea as the glaciers retreated some 430 million years ago during the Ordovician geologic period. As time passed, that iron-oxide bottom soil compressed into a type of rock called Queenston Shale, a major component of the nearby Niagara Escarpment. Ordovician shale underlies most of south-central Ontario, but only near the escarpment does it lie so close to the surface.

Pull off the surface vegetation, scrape the ground with your foot and there it is—red iron oxide. Chop trees, pull away too much vegetation and eventually weather will erode an entire area into a Martian land-scape, which is what happened north of Cheltenham at the start of the 20th century.

Poor farming practices—too many sheep probably, but it could have been cattle—caused overgrazing, and erosion did the rest. What you see at the Cheltenham Badlands took less than a century to accomplish, and is primarily the result of the hand of man. The prehistoric quality of the place is nothing but a mirage, a mirage that should be mandatory viewing for agricultural students and anyone interested in preserving what sustains life on this tiny planet called Earth: the soil.

FERTILIZER DEMYSTIFIED

Let's face it. Plants don't give a hoot if their nutrition comes from dried manure or the Acme Fertilizer Company. To plants, nitrogen, phosphorus, potassium and trace minerals are the same no matter what the source—their roots can only take up inorganic, water-soluble nutrients. What matters to the plant is that nutrients are present and in a ready-to-use form. That is the chief disadvantage of organic fertilizers—they need time to break down. On the other hand, you will not over-fertilize or burn the roots with organics and you will have better soil workability and water retention.

Another disadvantage to manure and the like is lack of information on the amount of nutrients in the product. Inorganic fertilizers come with three big numbers on the bag, so there is never a question of how much of what is in it. The first of those three numbers refers to the amount of nitrogen (N) in the product. Nitrogen is an element common in the atmosphere. Fertilizer production begins by mixing air with methane gas and subjecting both to heat, pressure and a catalyst to produce anhydrous ammonia, which when mixed with nitric acid produces nitrate fertilizers. More than 100 million tons of nitrate fertilizer is manufactured annually around the globe using almost 5% of natural gas production. Nitrates come in various purities, but for agricultural use, the content is 20% or lower, the first number on the fertilizer bag: 20. Nitrogen promotes plant growth and enables a healthy, dark green colour.

The second number on the bag refers to the element phosphorus (P), which is not found as a free element in nature. Agricultural phosphorus is made by mining phosphate rock, grinding it fine and treating it with sulfuric acid to produce water-soluble superphosphate. Deposits of bat and bird droppings are also mined for water-soluble phosphate. Phosphorous is a constituent of DNA, RNA and the cell walls of all living creatures. It is an essential element for life, and in plants it promotes root growth, flower and seed production, maturity and a healthy, dark green colour.

The third number on the fertilizer bag refers to the element potassium (K, from *kalium*, Latin for an Arabic word meaning "plant ashes"). The loose term "potash" refers to the mineral potassium carbonate and related mined or manufactured salts that contain water-soluble potassium. Potassium carbonate is used for for making glass and soap and leavening bread, potassium hydroxide (lye) for soap making and nitrate of potash (saltpetre) for making gunpowder. The potash employed as a fertilizer is potassium chloride, or muriate of potassium. This mineral is mined from ancient sea beds and clay deposits. Potassium is a necessary element for both people and plants, and Canada supplies the world with around one-third of its agricultural potash needs from mines in Saskatchewan. Plants need potassium to maintain moisture balance, resist disease, grow strong roots and issue large grain heads or flowers.

If you want big, bright flowers on healthy plants, use a fertilizer with a high middle number, but watch the burn. Never apply fertilizers to dry beds, and take special care when applying high middle number fertilizers to container plants.

At my golf and country club, we plant lots of geraniums, some in hanging baskets. We water baskets in the early morning and give them a heavy dose of high phosphate

fertilizer every four weeks (2 cups in 90 litres of water). Our baskets receive water every morning (water drains from the bottom) so only a small amount of fertilizer is retained by the plant roots. Never fertilize dry containers or soil, as it will burn tender plant roots; only apply to water-saturated soil. At the golf and country club, we fertilize flowerbeds and shrubs just before, during or immediately after rainstorms.

FACTS

Potash may contain high concentrations of naturally occurring uranium; the uptake of this potash may result in radioactive crops.

The German alchemist Hennig Brand discovered phosphorus in 1675 while he searched for traces of gold in unusual natural products, like his own urine.

There are two types of phosphorus, white and red, and both saw use in the manufacture of match heads. Cheaper to manufacture, white phosphorus was commonly used in matches, but because of high toxicity production was discontinued over time beginning in 1906.

Symptoms of Nutrient Deficiency in Plants

- *Nitrogen:* yellowing leaves, stunted growth and dropped leaves
- *Phosphorous:* stunted, dark colour of first leaves
- *Potassium:* yellowing leaves beginning with oldest
- *Calcium:* malformed leaves and blackened ends of fruit

- **Magnesium:** discoloration between veins
- **Sulphur:** stunted plants and yellowing of young leaves
- **Iron:** yellowing between veins.

The nutrients listed above are necessary to keep plants healthy and happy, but other micro and macro mineral elements can enhance the growing ability of plants, and then there are the bio-stimulants. Bio-stimulants are naturally occurring minerals and organics not considered essential for plant development, but are recognized enhancers of plant growth and health and used extensively by commercial growers. Most bio-stimulants are available to home gardeners.

Triacontanol, also known melissyl alcohol, is a naturally occurring plant hormone found in beeswax that is capable of boosting a plant's ability to photosynthesize sunlight. You add tiny amounts to the fertilizer or foliar feed and—presto—you have a bigger, healthier plant.

Humates, humic and fulvic acids are found in peat, compost piles and a low-grade coal known as leonardite. These naturally occurring chemicals can promote fantastic growth in plants, especially the fulvic acid. Fulvic acid affects plant membranes and improves uptake of nutrients as well increased photosynthesis. Humates work especially well with hydroponic systems and are widely used in commercial installations for both flowers and vegetable production. Humates are best added to soil or liquid feed, as plant roots take them up and send to new growth to aid photosynthesis. They also aid in root formation and contribute to the overall health of the plant.

Amino acids derived from plant soy can have a dramatic effect on plant growth when foliar fed or added to soil. When added to soil, amino acids benefit local

micro-flora, increase nutrient uptake by plant roots and contribute to the overall health of plants.

Common aspirin (acetylsalicylic acid), when added to soil, exhibits a hormone-like quality that aids in flowering, disease resistance and root formation. Aspirin is a tried-and-true disease fighter for plants because it induces a resistance to various plant maladies. Prepare by dissolving up to 2 uncoated tablets per gallon of water.

While the rest of the world spends anywhere from 20 to 50% of their disposable income on food, Canadians fork out only around 10%, and fertilizers must be credited for the blessing. Our farmers are productive because they know the value of soil testing and they get support from government agencies and the fertilizer companies. To a farmer, soil is family, and knowing the health of family members is paramount to their survival. Farmers know exactly what ails the soil and how to fix it, and if not all they need to do is pick up the phone a call an expert. Home gardeners are small-scale farmers, and they can access the same help lines as the commercial operations. If you have a question regarding fertilizer, pick up a phone and call an expert or go online, as most pertinent information is posted.

Soil testing is important to farmers and gardeners alike; farmers test from various sites in their fields and at various depths using boring tools. Home gardeners need not go to such lengths, but following the directions of the testing laboratory to the letter is crucial.

Improved farming practices, such as soil testing, starter fertilizers and pinpoint timing of major fertilizer applications, have seen Canadian farmers almost triple crop yields since the 1960s, and with less fertilizer. The home gardener need only emulate the farmer to achieve similar results. Remember, your garden soil does not naturally contain all of the minerals needed for optimum yields; you must add them into the soil in a manner most useful to crops.

Also, keep in mind that rotation is beneficial to plants. For example, do not plant your tomatoes in the same place every year because they seem to belong in that spot; move them around to a different place each year. If you employ raised beds, move the tomatoes into another bed, and they will thank you with loads of big, juicy tomatoes. Beans you can leave, since they bring their own grub to the party (fixing nitrogen) but all the others need moving around—and don't forget those beans need other nutrients besides nitrogen.

FACTS

Canada produces around 24 million tons of fertilizer annually and the industry contributes about $6 billion to the national economy.

Contrary to popular belief, the ingredients in fertilizer are all natural products and identical to nutrients found in manure and compost.

Fertilizer is Canada's largest export to India, with 2008 sales showing an increase of 287.5 % over 2007.

BIG STUFF

Giant Pumpkins

They will put on around 18 kilograms every day and during their four-and-a-half month growing season will drink up 4000 gallons of water. They feed on exotic fertilizers, grow on vines trimmed daily and are protected from sun and rain like babies. They are the patented, Atlantic Giant variety of competition pumpkins, and one seed from a world champion can sell for upwards of $500. World champions have been surpassing the current year's record for more than a decade and in 2008, the species reached an incredible 696.95 kilograms. That year was a furious one for champions, as dozens of annual fall weigh-ins saw world records fall like snow in February. In the end, when all the dust of excitement had settled, a Canadian pumpkin claimed the title of Grand Champion and world record holder at the Elk Grove Giant Pumpkin and Harvest Festival in Elk Grove, California. The grower, Jake Van Kooten of Port Alberni, BC, took home a prize of almost $10,000 and stands to make much more from the sale of seeds.

Making money and having fun is always an enviable endeavour, so why not plant a big one and go for the gusto. You will need seeds, and there is only one variety worth considering—the late Howard Dill's patented Atlantic Giant variety.

Howard Dill hailed from Windsor, NS, and single-handedly brought to life Charles Schulz's "Great Pumpkin" from the Snoopy cartoons. Howard taught himself genetics and spent years crossing different plants until he arrived at a recognized variety he called Atlantic Giant. During the early 1980s, he grew a world record 181 kilogram giant, and growers sat up and took notice. Howard broke his own record four times in successive years and inspired his hometown Pumpkin Regatta, where participants race rowboats carved from pumpkins. Known around the world as the Pumpkin King, Howard passed away in 2008, but his company, Howard Dill Enterprises, is still in the business of selling seeds. The company takes online orders, but you must be quick because seeds of the current champion sell out quickly. Howard Dill Enterprises also offers free online expertise in the process of growing a big one. If having the Great Pumpkin rise up from your patch sounds like fun, you should grow the Atlantic Giant.

Remember, when you buy seeds for giant vegetables or fruits, make sure they are "open pollinated," which means they are not hybridized and will produce the same variety of fruit or vegetable year after year. Also keep in mind that drip irrigation works best—these giants need a constant supply of water.

Giant Squash

While not as popular as pumpkins, the giant squash still has legions of aficionados. Their variety of choice is the Show King Giant Green developed by Howard Dill, of giant pumpkin fame. Growing giant squash requires diligent attention to water, food, insect pests and weather. They need full sun, plenty of water, lots of fertilizer and rich, well-drained soil. Keeping them watered is important, and the soil must be soaked thoroughly. Fertilizer is a matter of preference, but most growers use a combination of brand name and fish emulsion. There will be no going away from this task—no weekend trips, no visiting Aunt Martha, zero, not for four months, because if the weather turns hot and you miss a watering, the Frankenstein's monster in your garden could suddenly slow down its growth or even stop growing altogether.

Getting them big is also a matter of luck, because squash are not frost hardy. An early frost in spring or fall means your squash is kaput. Experienced growers of humungous squash and pumpkins construct cloches or small PVC-swathed houses and are ready for frost events. In hot, humid weather, the experienced grower looks for fungus or bacterial infection—powdery mildew and bacterial wilt being the most common—and they are ready with a fungicide and wilt treatment. Doing everything right, and if the weather is on your side for a change, you could have a half-ton monster in your garden in around 130 days. A good-looking monster too, because Howard Dill's Show Kings are a nice shade of greyish green and will make you proud as punch come the fall weigh-in. Buying seeds is always a problem because the good champion stock always sell out quickly, so plan ahead and be first in line for next year's seed. For information on planting, see the Howard Dill website.

Giant Gourds

The grower's choice for producing a 3.5 metre, bathtub-sized calabash is Giant Long Gourd, and another is the African Wine Kettle, the giant bushel gourd. Unlike pumpkins and squash, gourds are not fussy about soil conditions, although they prefer soil to be well drained with a pH between 5.9 and 6.3. Giant varieties take around 130 days to mature, so in Canada it is better to start seeds indoors and transplant to the garden when the threat of frost has passed. One hundred pound gourds are standard and when dried will weigh around 10 pounds. They make delightful painted furniture.

Giant Watermelon

Carolina Cross is the variety of watermelon that produces 50 kilogram giants with little effort by growers. However, if you are like Bill Edwards of Michigan, a lot of effort can yield a world record 121.11 kilogram behemoth.

FACTS

Pumpkins, squash and gourds belong to the genus *Cucurbita* and are plagued by sucking and boring insects. Many growers of giant *Cucurbita* treat seeds and spray with a Bayer-manufactured nicotine insecticide called Admire that is widely used by potato growers. The active ingredient in Admire is "imidacloprid," a chemical only mildly toxic to humans.

Beware of the inert delivery agents in Admire, as both crystalline quartz silica and naphthalene are recognized carcinogens.

Pumpkins are fruit, not vegetable, and are 90% water.

On April 17, 2007, the state of Oklahoma passed a bill declaring watermelon the official state vegetable. In Oklahoma, watermelon is no longer fruit, but a vegetable. Hang up yur 10-gallon, partner, 'cause we got steak and watermelon for supper.

Over 1200 varieties of watermelon are grown in over 100 countries.

Watermelons are a healthy food: they are high in fibre, contain no fat or cholesterol and are a good source of vitamins A, C and potassium.

Giant Tomatoes

The varieties to choose for kilo-sized fruit are Old Colossus Heirloom, Giant Belgium, Big Zac or Burpee's Supersteak. Tomato plants are self-pollinating—the flowers contain both male and female organs, and any movement by wind or vibration is enough to transfer pollen. Not so with the big boy flowers, as they are too large and will need help pollinating from either a friendly honeybee or the grower. Pollinating is easy. Just pick a flower during the middle of the day and rub the cone against the stigma of another flower. Remove smaller flowers from the cluster and allow the fruit to set for the months of June and July. By August remove all but the largest fruit. Prune at the end of July, down to a single vine or main stem from a secondary branch.

Giant tomato plants are both hungry and thirsty and will need lots of fertilizer and water. Many growers use a mixture of commercial fertilizer and seaweed/fish emulsion, and finding the combination that works for you is part of the fun.

Giant Onions

Kelsae Sweet Giants always hold world records; the current one is 7.49 kilograms.

Sunflowers

The tallest sunflower shot up in the Netherlands to reach a height of 7.76 metres, and Emily Martin of Maple Ridge, BC, grew the plant with the largest head. The seed to get for monstrous sunflowers with over 0.5 metre sized heads is Grey Stripes Giant.

Giant Cucumbers

The seed to get is Mammoth Zeppelin, and it is called that for good reason. According to Guinness, the world's longest, and still growing, is a 1.2 metre dirigible-sized fruit belonging to English bus driver Yitzhak Yizdanpana. Yitzy claims he did nothing special to get the monster to such a size, but he is probably keeping secrets.

The heaviest cucumber, grown in Australia in 1988, tipped the scales at a fantastic 26.8 kilograms.

I am not a big fan of cucumbers, and seeing one is to be reminded of the recipe for tasteless cukes put forward by the famed author and wit, Dr. Samuel Johnson: "A cucumber should be well sliced, and dressed with pepper and vinegar, and then thrown out as good for nothing."

Giant Cabbages

You can make a lot of coleslaw with a 50 kilogram cabbage, and if weather treats you well, that is what you can expect from a seed called Northern Giant. English seed and plant breeder Dr. Bernard Lavery grew a 56.24 kilogram monster during the early 90s that took up an area 6 by 7 metres and broke a world's record that stands today. Dr. Lavery's secret required setting several PVC pipes into the ground to get nutrients to the giant's roots. He probably has many more secrets, but like all growers of behemoth veggies, he is keeping mum.

Giant Carrots

The seed you want is called Japanese Imperial Long Carrot. The heaviest to date of this variety weighed in at a whopping 8.6 kilograms and was grown in 1998, by John Evans of Palmer, Alaska.

Some Big Things to Inspire

- The world's biggest tree is a sequoia growing in California's Sequoia National Park. Affectionately called the General Sherman, the large sequoia is 83.82 metres tall and reported to be the largest tree on the planet.

- The world's fastest-growing plant is a bamboo species *Bambusa oldhamii,* with a reported growth rate of 91 centimetres per day.

- A tree with the all-time greatest circumference grows on the slopes of Mt Etna, in Sicily. Known as the Tree of a Hundred Horses, this monster European chestnut (*Castanea sativa*) was officially measured in 1780. It had a girth of 57.9 metres, from whence comes the hundred horses name, as that many would be needed to surround the beast. A tough nut, the tree has survived volcanic eruptions, war and old age, but over the centuries has broken into three parts and no longer qualifies as a world record breaker.

- The largest edible fungi, a giant puffball *Calvatia gigantea* found by Jean-Guy Richard of Montreal in 1987, weighed a hefty 22 kilograms and had a circumference of 2.64 metres.

- The world's largest forest is the great boreal belt in northern Russia with an area of 1.1 billion hectares.

- The largest fruit tree collection is at Brogdale, Kent, in the UK. It consists of 4500 trees, including 2300 varieties of apple trees.

- The world's largest garden, created by André Le Notre for Louis XIV in the late 17th century out of swampland in Versailles, France, encompasses some 15,000 acres.

- The plants with the largest leaves are the raffia palm (*Raphia farinifera*), native to the Mascarene Islands in the Indian Ocean, and the Amazonian bamboo palm (*R. taedigera*), native to Africa and South America. Both have leaves in excess of 20 metres.

- The world's largest seed belongs to the giant fan palm (*Lodoicea maldivica*). Commonly know as the coco de mer, a single seed from this tree can weigh 20 kilograms and take 10 years to develop.

- The world's largest weed is the giant hogweed (*Heracleum mantegazzianum*). Imported from the Caucasus to Europe, the U.S. and Canada as an ornamental in the 18th century, the weed can grow to almost 4 metres in height.

- The world's heaviest lemon, grown by Aharon Shemoel on his farm in Israel, tipped the scales at a fantastic 5.265 kilos.

- The world's slowest growing tree is a white cedar (*Thuja occidentalis*) found on a cliffside on Ontario's Niagara Escarpment. Measured and weighed at regular intervals over a period of 150 years, the tree has grown to a height of 10.2 centimetres and weighs 17 grams.

HERBS

Medicinal Herbs

Most people who cook are aware of the taste advantages obtained by adding herbs to food preparations, but common kitchen herbs are but a sliver of the vast number used for medicinal purposes. Chinese doctors have used herbs beneficially for thousands of years, a fact ignored by traditional medical practitioners until only recently. Traditional Chinese medicine practitioners, unlike their western counterparts who address the symptoms of disease, will go after the root cause with a variety of treatments, such as herbal medicines, acupuncture and shiatsu massage. Oriental medical practitioners also hold to the belief that optimum human health can only be achieved by keeping a proper balance within the body (qi) and imbalances may be restored through nutrition, medicinal herbs, exercise and meditation.

The bibles of traditional Oriental medicine are the 2000-year-old *Shen Nong's Herbal Classic* and the *Great Pharmacopoeia* published in the 16th century. *Shen Nong's Herbal Classic* classifies hundreds of cures into three categories. Superior includes herbs good for multiple ailments and useful for restoring balance to the body. The second category lists herb tonics and health boosters meant to be consumed in the short term. The third category lists herbs consumed in tiny amounts and for specific ailments.

Shen Nong's number-one superior herb is a mushroom with magical properties. The lingzhi mushroom (reishi in Japanese; *Ganoderma lucidum*), is the Geritol tonic of the Orient and the only known source of ganoderic acid, a plant terpene with a molecular structure similar to steroid hormones. The mushroom also contains biologically active polysaccharides thought to be potent cancer fighters. Of this mushroom, *Shen Nong's Herbal Classic* states:

> The taste is bitter, its energy neutral, it has no toxicity. It cures the accumulation of pathogenic factor in the chest. It is good for the qi of the head including mental activities. Long-term consumption will lighten the body; you will never become old. It lengthens years.

Does it really? Maybe, as studies have found the mushroom has anticancer, immunoregularity, antioxidant, antiviral, antibacterial, antifungal and antifibrotic properties. Almost as bonus, an extract of the mushroom will increase endurance for physical and sexual activities. As Shen Nong promised, it is an all-round tonic and health booster, but as yet nobody knows if it will add years to your life.

If a healthier, longer life interests you, then check out your local woodlots and forests, because the *Ganoderma* mushroom of Asian fame also grows right here in Canada. How that happens nobody is quite sure—it may be a native species, or it may have hitched a ride with Chinese railway workers. How it got here is not important; what is important is what it can do for your health, because live and fresh is far better than dried, packaged and shipped last year from questionable sources.

Canada is home to other medicinal mushrooms said to provide medicinal benefit. The maitake ("dancing") mushroom (*Grifola frondosa*) will, according to studies, boost your immune system and stabilize both blood sugar and pressure. Another more common medicinal

'shroom is turkey tail (*Trametes versicolor*), which contains a polysaccharide called krestin that is being used in cancer therapy. Then there is chaga (*Inonotus obliquus*), an ugly 'shroom that hangs from birch trees like an insect infestation, but packs a medicinal punch that contains all manner of chemicals known to fight cancer and invigorate the body. If you think hunting up medicinal mushrooms is your thing, get some books on the subject and study hard, because in the world of wild mushroom foraging, mistakes are frowned upon, usually by an examining physician.

If overcome by an inclination to grow medicinal herbs, you should first clarify the why before deciding what to grow. If something specific is ailing you, see a medical doctor, naturopath or Chinese herbalist. Since the use of herbs is generally considered a tonic or preventive against specific ailments, using medicinal herbs for specific ailments is best left to experts. Disclaimer done with, here is a list of medicinal herbs worth considering for a patch in your garden:

Aloe (*Aloe vera*): good for burns and cuts, the thick juice is squeezed from a leaf and applied to wound like any other salve.

Chamomile (*Chamaemelum nobile*): dried, this herb makes a relaxing tea to aid in restful sleep.

Dill (*Anethum graveolens*) or dillweed: both a medicinal and culinary herb good for fish dishes. If your tummy is aching or upset, a teaspoon in hot water will soon have you right as rain. Dill is the main ingredient in gripe water, every mother's best friend for colicky babies.

French Tarragon (*Artemisia dracunculus*): goes well with chicken, fish, rice dishes and salads. It has slight anesthetic properties and will also calm a toothache.

Lavender (*Lavalandula angustifolia*): dried, the flowers and stems make an invigorating room freshener, while the seeds placed into sachets make a marvelous freshener for linens and closets. Lavender oil has antiseptic properties and is used in creams and ointments for healing minor wounds and abrasions.

OIL INFUSION

Finely chop dried herbs and combine with 3 cups olive oil in a glass bowl. Place bowl over a saucepan of boiling water, turn down heat and simmer for 2 to 3 hours. Strain through cheesecloth or jelly bag into a storage bottle and keep in a dark cool place.

Lemon Balm (*Melissa officinalis*): dried, this herb makes a healing tea for upset stomachs.

St. John's Wort (*Hypericum perforatum*): dried and infused with olive oil, this herb heals burns, abrasions and rashes.

Culinary Herbs
THE MINT FAMILY

Basil (*Ocimum basilicum*): an herb once thought purely medicinal until the tomato arrived in Europe. When cooks discovered the wonderful relationship between the two, they began to cultivate in earnest. All you need to grow basil is a container—it is a prodigious grower. Several small pots will suffice to keep you supplied all summer.

Lavender (*Lavalandula angustifolia*): the original soul food, as nothing energizes the spirit like the rich aroma of this herb. Lavender stems and flowers contain glands that secrete the fragrant oil with so many uses: soap, potpourris to scent linen closets, bath oil, flavouring for candy, meats, stews, jams and jellies. Easy to grow, but like all members

of the mint family it can become an invasive weed and is best grown in containers, raised beds or a parterre.

Mint (*Mentha* spp.): another soul restorative used in jellies and sauces and to make one of the most refreshing teas on the planet. Mint is easy to grow, but is best confined to containers or raised beds, because it can become nasty and take over your entire garden.

Oregano (*Origanum vulgare*): an herb widely used in Italian cookery and a revelation for cooks who have never tried it fresh. The dried store-bought variety is actually a variety of wild Mexican marjoram with none of the pizzazz and taste of the fresh.

Parsley (*Petroselinum crispum*): you can never have enough of this wonderful herb. It comes in two varieties, French and Italian, with the former being the Canadian favourite. Cooks find this herb a must-have in the garden and I recommend a good-sized planting.

Rosemary (*Rosmarinus officinalis*): both a culinary and aromatic herb, this plant does well in containers of any size, but a large one is recommended owing its restorative aroma.

Thyme (*Thymus* spp.): another aromatic widely used to flavour meats and sauces. Thyme does extremely well in rock gardens and other hard-to-grow places, and makes a nifty groundcover.

THE ONIONS

There are two types of globe-shaped onions—spring/summer, and storage, or cooking onions. The former is grown in warmer climates, the latter in cooler climes, like Canada. Storage onions are more pungent than their sweeter, southern cousins, and when allowed to dry a few months attain a crisp, paper-like skin. Many *Allium* species are also used for their tasty leaves.

No cook can get along without a supply of fresh chives. Chives are perennial *Alliums* grown from bulbs, and the easiest way to get some into your garden is by transferring a clump from a friend's garden. Barring that, just plant some seeds. They like containers of any size and will do well as long as they have full sun and do not dry out. Several medium-sized containers planted with chives are best, with harvested shoots cut to the ground for regeneration into fresh vibrant new shoots. In late spring, the plant produces purple flowers—remove them immediately because they interfere with shoot growth. Chives prefer a rich, damp soil in full sun and are best harvested with sharp scissors. Snip, snip and pass the cream cheese and bagels.

Scallions, green onions and spring onions are all immature seedling onions picked before they mature. They do well in raised beds, but require rich, well-drained soil and full sun. Almost any onion can be a scallion—plant as early in the spring as possible and when the shoots are about 20 centimetres tall dig them up and voilà, green onion tops and scallion bottoms.

FACTS

Onions contain phenols, flavonoids and phyto-nutrients that protect against cardiovascular disease and cancer, especially liver and colon cancer. Sweet onions contain the least amount of these beneficial chemicals, while shallots contain the most.

According to the Environmental Working Group's 2009 report, *Shopper's Guide to Pesticides*, onions contain the least pesticide residues of 47 foods and vegetables tested by the USDA and FDA. Peaches contain the most.

WEIRD GARDEN STORY

Sir William Cornelius Builds a Country

Railways made this country. To understand why and how, we have to consider the American railway experience beginning with the Civil War. That war began on a level playing field; the North had the industrial might, but the South had agricultural muscle with easy access to the sea and European markets. In 1861, at the outset of the war, the U.S. had 50,000 kilometres of rail track, with less than one-third under Southern control. Northern rail lines ran west to the Ohio and Mississippi river valleys and featured many trunk lines. Southern rail lines connected the Atlantic seaboard with the Mississippi River, with trunk lines running out of Chattanooga and Richmond. Take out those terminal cities, and the South's military muscle would wilt for lack of supplies; a fact the Confederacy was slow to comprehend until General William T. Sherman showed up at the gates of Richmond.

Railways helped the North get men and supplies to where they were needed quickly. Railways won the war for the North, and they emerged from the fracas as a driving force behind U.S. expansionism. A year after the guns opened up in 1861, the U.S. Congress, at the urging of President Lincoln, implemented the Homestead and Pacific Railway acts that provided settlers outside of the 13 Northern states with 160-acre parcels of farmland and a way to get there. The Homestead Act fairly guaranteed the West's support for the Northern cause, and at war's end in 1865 over 200 million acres had been claimed by settlers, and the railway had passed through Omaha, Nebraska, on the way to the coast. President Lincoln had considered it expedient to American interests to continue laying track to the coast to quell the threat of a California succession from the Union.

Only the venture was extremely costly and he initially found no takers for the project, because little opportunity existed to recoup investment. Lincoln needed a carrot to entice the railway barons, and he thought if deeding land to homesteaders had worked so well, why not try it on the railroads (no sweat off his brow—the land did not even belong to the Union of States). So it was that two railways—the Central Pacific, which started east from California in 1862, and the Union Pacific, which started west in 1865—received land grants totalling 200 million acres. Most of this land was sold off to arriving settlers. Railways became big business, and by 1880 around 1000 railways operated in the U.S., and one in particular, the Northern Pacific, was busily laying track into Canada.

In his 1997 book, *Manifest Destiny and Western Canada*, noted author Todd D. Sauve claims the building of the Northern Pacific, along with the Indian wars and the construction of Fort Abraham Lincoln in North Dakota, were preludes to an invasion of Canada by a victorious Union army wanting to clear the continent of British influence. The British Parliament took the threat so seriously that in 1862 they ordered their military commanders to draw up contingency plans to thwart such an incursion. Residents of Nova Scotia, New Brunswick and Canada East and West were doubly convinced an invasion was imminent when in 1866, the U.S. House of Representatives passed an act allowing for the admission of those "new states" into the Union, and the U.S. Congress cancelled the Canadian-American Reciprocity Treaty, an act that allowed for trade without tariffs. U.S. invasion was a real threat, but probably never saw implementation for three reasons: the assassination of President Lincoln, the unforeseen military fortitude of the Plains Indians, and the almost complete destruction of the U.S. naval fleet during the Civil War.

However, all these events instilled fear into our forefathers, who put several things into motion that would ultimately benefit Canada: among them Confederation and the building of our own transcontinental railway, the Canadian Pacific. The newly formed Canada had no choice but to build the railway, because in 1871 British Columbia made its completion within 10 years a condition of joining Confederation. Sir John A. Macdonald, Canada's first prime minister, in his zeal to have the railway built, got his Conservative Party involved in a kick-back scandal that lost him the 1873 election to Alexander Mackenzie's Liberal Party. Mackenzie wanted no part of building railways, and construction stopped until the next election in 1878, when Macdonald was re-elected.

Back in office, Sir John A. decided the best way to show British Columbia he meant business was to concentrate construction in that province and for that, an American contractor, Andrew Onderdonk was hired to oversee construction. Onderdonk had never built a railway, but he had successfully completed construction of the San Francisco seawall, as formable a task as ramming rail through the Rocky Mountains. Onderdonk took a page from the Union Pacific and hired cheap Chinese workers. When Onderdonk ran short of local Chinese, he imported workers from China. At the height of construction he had 15,000 Chinese workers doing everything from laying track to blasting tunnels. Hundreds died, usually from premature explosions as they prepared black powder charges. Onderdonk even emulated Union Pacific's method of feeding his workers; he provided rice and hired hunters to kill wild game. While crossing the American plains, Union Pacific hunters killed thousands of buffalo, but in the Rocky Mountains Onderdonk's workers were not so lucky and often ate only rice and found greens.

There is a story that Union Pacific's cheap labour combo, Chinese workers fed hunted buffalo meat, was an idea formulated by President Ulysses S. Grant to counter his problem with Native Peoples. Starving the Confederate army during the Civil War had been largely his idea, and if it worked once, it might work again on the warring tribes of the American plains. His orders to kill all the buffalo within the railway right-of-way was interpreted by hunters to mean anywhere the buffalo roamed; within a decade their numbers had dwindled from millions to thousands. However, this action backfired. It so infuriated the tribes they donned war paint, and the resulting Indian wars cost the U.S. government $25 million annually for decades.

But back to Andrew Onderdonk, who did not have a problem with warring tribes. Over the next few years Andrew continued the building of 545 kilometres of track through difficult, mountainous terrain to into Craigellachie, BC.

With the west to east railway underway, Sir John could concentrate on the east to west construction. A group of investors with rail-building experience had already come forward, and on February 16, 1881, the Canadian Pacific Railway was official recognized and was awarded a grant of $25 million along with 25 million acres of land to encourage construction. But after one disappointing year of construction, with a little better than 200 kilometres of track laid, the CPR hired an American railway man, William Cornelius Van Horne, as general manager. Van Horne soon had the rails headed west at breakneck speed, and by August of 1883,

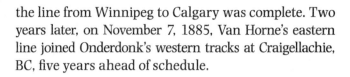

the line from Winnipeg to Calgary was complete. Two years later, on November 7, 1885, Van Horne's eastern line joined Onderdonk's western tracks at Craigellachie, BC, five years ahead of schedule.

Van Horne was made vice-president of the CPR and could now concentrate his talents on making money for the investors, a thing he accomplished at his customary breakneck speed by turning the infrastructure of building a railway into commercial enterprises: the telegraph, lumber supply, surveyors and food stores all got popped into whistle stops along with a railway detective. Van Horne's new game was selling off parcels of the 25 million acre government grant. The CPR got into the real estate business big time, and to secure customers they advertised in European newspapers.

The response was immediate and almost overwhelming. Immigrants arrived by the shipload, but Van Horne was ready with land, cheaply built hotels, transportation to their farms, lumber and a way to contact home for more money. That money rolled in so fast he had to open banks to keep it safe while investing in wheat seeds to give the new farmers. His seeds were the Red Fife spring wheat variety planted in the rest of Canada and the U.S., and hard-as-nails durum wheat, a variety used in Italy to produce macaroni. Van Horne had already investigated their potential and knew the future of the railway lay in those varieties of yellow gold. Van Horne instructed the CPR to facilitate their introduction to prairie farmers by offering to ship seed stock free.

In 1888, Van Horne became president of the CPR and was virtual lord and master of a transportation juggernaut that changed the face of an entire nation. The CPR built and serviced its own rolling stock and in 1891 launched its own ships, the Empress Line. On the prairies, the Red Fife and durum wheat crop yields surpassed even Van Horne's expectations. The stuff grew like wildfire and began piling up at whistle stops, so he built special grain elevators and charged farmers storage and grading fees on top of transport costs. For a price, the CPR would even sell the wheat and loan farmers money on next year's crop.

Van Horne was a man for all seasons; he even dabbled in architecture and gardening. He helped design the Banff Springs and Château Frontenac hotels. He delighted in showing off their spectacular flower gardens to friends and visitors, the flowers personally selected by him on visits to Holland. In 1894, Van Horne became Sir William Cornelius Van Horne; not bad for a kid from Chelsea, Illinois, who began working on the railway at age 14. Self-educated, driven to perfection and the maker of almost everything Canadian, Van Horne retired from the presidency of the CPR in 1899 to become that line's first chairman, a job with little responsibility.

Van Horne had become a very wealthy man, but once a railway man, always a railway man, so off he went off to Cuba to build more track. Van Horne died at Montreal on September 11, 1915, and two nations mourned his passing. In Canada the flag flew at half-mast in Ottawa and the CPR ceased operations for the day, and Cuba declared a national day of mourning for Sir William Cornelius Van Horne, our nation builder, our Mister Canada.

FACTS

One pound of supermarket lettuce contains around 80 calories. Growing, processing and shipping that amount of lettuce uses up approximately 5000 calories of fossil fuel energy.

Fredrick Law Olmsted, the famous American landscape architect who designed New York City's Central Park, also designed Mount Royal Park in Montreal. One of Olmsted's protégés, Henry A. Engelhardt, immigrated to Canada and won several large garden commissions, including the Ontario Agricultural College at Guelph, and Toronto's famed Mount Pleasant Cemetery.

CANADA UNDER GLASS

Around 30 AD, the Roman emperor Tiberius had an early form of greenhouse, called a *specularium*, erected to provide him with an endless supply of salad greens and grapes. To let the light in—glass panes not yet having been invented—sheets of the translucent mineral mica were set into mortar, producing a result resembling stained glass windows. Heat for the specularium came from radiant heating, a rather advanced concept for the times: a fire pit in the basement heated the concrete floor and warmed the air. He must have started a fad, because archaeologists have been unearthing specularia all over Italy.

Several centuries later, in 1599, a French botanist named Jules Charles constructed the first glass hothouse in Leiden, Holland, ostensibly to grow medicinal herbs imported from the tropics, but he also planted tropical fruit trees which became something of a sensation. The first greenhouse attracted lots of attention, especially on weekends when townspeople and visitors lined up to sample whatever fruit had ripened on the trees. Charles even offered sweetened fruit drinks, tamarind and guava being the favourites.

But it was the orange from China that set off the European greenhouse craze; called orangeries, and they became a must-have addition to every noble's château or manor house. Some orangeries were huge; Tsar Alexander of Russia built three that were over 213 metres long and almost 14 metres high.

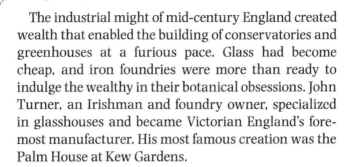

The industrial might of mid-century England created wealth that enabled the building of conservatories and greenhouses at a furious pace. Glass had become cheap, and iron foundries were more than ready to indulge the wealthy in their botanical obsessions. John Turner, an Irishman and foundry owner, specialized in glasshouses and became Victorian England's foremost manufacturer. His most famous creation was the Palm House at Kew Gardens.

Ships ventured out from England to scour the globe for new and exciting fruit and flowering plants; many funded by two famous garden supply families, the Veitch family in England, and the Vilmorins of France. The Vilmorins stocked greenhouses around the world with exotic plant life, including those constructed in 19th-century Halifax, Montreal and Toronto.

In Canada, commercial gardening under glass or plastic over the years has turned from a pastime of the wealthy to a business, with around 21 million square metres in production. About 10% is concentrated in the area around Leamington, Ontario. Flowers and nursery stock account for around 65% of volume, and vegetables make up the remainder. Tomatoes are almost half the vegetable production, followed by cucumber, peppers and lettuce. Business is booming for growers, and every year since 1990 has seen increases in production and sales.

Homeowners have also been flocking to glass or plastic houses, and the selection is vast. Gardeners considering building a greenhouse must first decide on the purpose of the building. Do you want to grow vegetables, to over-winter garden plants, orchids or tropicals, to have a mixed usage or just to have another room on the house?

As a former owner/operator of a garden centre that featured a large greenhouse, I am constantly leaned on for advice. Mostly the questions come from friends or associates who already have a small greenhouse and want to upgrade to a larger installation. I get asked questions like, should I use glass or polycarbonate plastic? Attached to the house or freestanding? South facing or east? Oil or gas heat? Can I include a hot tub? And, probably the most important question...how big? Answering questions is easy if I know the people and their reasons for wanting a first or upgraded green-house. Not knowing you, I will assume the greenhouse is a first venture and will advise accordingly.

Expense and space are the main concerns. Can you afford to build a greenhouse that is right for you, and do you have the necessary footage? If the answer is no to either question, then do not even consider a proper greenhouse and go with a kit. I am not a big fan of small kits, or prefabricated greenhouses, but some gardeners are quite happy working in a plastic hut. The problem with these kits is just that, the problems—the same problems with small as with big, only compounded. Sunshine heats the air quicker, the exhaust fan kicks in and there goes your humidity. People will usually not invest in a backup generator for a small green-house, and a power failure will cause all manner of troubles. In addition, small kit greenhouses usually lack a foundation, and high winds turn them into kites quicker than you can shake a stick. However, substan-tial kits are now on the market that will do a new glass-house gardener quite nicely; they are more expensive than tiny kits but they are still much less pricey than custom-built houses.

What I do recommend to homeowners is a conserva-tory or solarium—a room addition that will add value to the home. Normally not for the serious horticulturist, a solarium can be the best of both worlds and loads of fun. Load it up with plants, install a hot tub and have a small work area with a sink. Alternatively, you can

turn a solarium into a serious affair by installing shelves, a larger work area with two sinks and a potting table. It would be a serious greenhouse, and if you ever decide to sell the house, it can quickly be transformed into a page from *Architectural Digest*.

Of course, nothing beats the esthetically pleasing single-pane glass greenhouse. It is how we imagine the proper greenhouse to be, perhaps with a gothic arch. Nice, but our Canadian winters suck heat through those single panes almost as fast as the price of fuel rises. However, there are ways to have your cake and eat it too: double or triple-pane glazing is more expensive than single pane, but in the end will pay for itself many times over. Coupled with an interior insulation of PVC plastic or a painted-on coating, multi-paned glazing will lower heating costs considerably.

Solar Greenhouses

On sunny days, greenhouses collect solar energy that is dissipated by mechanical means, fans, opening roof vents, or a combination. With energy costs so high, allowing heat to escape is akin to throwing money away. There are two ways to save heat. A passive method uses items that heat can sink into during daylight and radiate at night, such as rocks, cement structures, walkways, a deep layer of gravel or crushed brick, and water barrels. An active system uses power to pump trapped heat into a lower storage area filled with rocks, large aggregate gravel or water barrels. The active system is more expensive, but it is far more efficient, especially in larger greenhouses.

Heat sinks are the items or structures that will store your heat during the day and release it at night. The most common heat sinks are the ubiquitous 55-gallon steel drums filled with water and painted flat black so as not to reflect heat. In smaller greenhouses, water barrels can support shelving and line walls, while in slightly larger houses, the barrels can be set on their sides in metal racks and piled three layers high. These heat sinks work, but not nearly as well as in an active system, where the greenhouse has a basement filled with barrels and heat is pumped down and around by fans. Active systems are more expensive to build, but the savings in power are huge and the extra effort will probably pay for itself in 10 years. Even more expensive, but vastly superior to bulky water barrels, is sodium sulfate decahydrate, or Glauber's salt, a chemical that melts at 32.2° C. Glauber's salt can be placed into black metal tubes and used in either a passive or an active manner. During daylight hours, sunshine will melt the Glauber's salt, causing it to absorb heat; at night, the salt will freeze at 32.2° C and release the stored heat. This "eutectic system" works so well you will have plenty of room in the greenhouse basement for storage or a workroom.

My grandfather raised orchids and employed both passive and active heating systems in a large, single-pane glazed greenhouse attached to the house. He used steam to heat the house and simply installed a larger boiler to facilitate the greenhouse. It was a common enough practice in those days, but his passive heating system was anything but common—the entire middle of the greenhouse was given over to a massive concrete structure that supported a 10,000 litre lake. The structure was both a delight and horror to his grandchildren, because in that lake were fish to control algae and something to keep their populations in check, a rather large alligator. That gator was actually the delight part—the horror lived in a long room under the lake, his army of insect eaters: camelback crickets. To small children, nothing is as horrifying as a dark, dank room with a ceiling covered in big, ugly spiders, and those crickets looked exactly like spiders. How they got there was a mystery, but since they only roamed

around at night and did a good job keeping the place free of insect pests, my granddad left them alone. Whenever we tried his patience with our endless questions, he would turn on the basement's single bare light bulb and show us the crickets. One look would have us tripping over ourselves in a frantic, screaming effort to leave the premises. Oh, about the alligator: it eventually grew to over 2 metres and was hauled out from the tank and presented to an aquarium society.

Solar Roof

For the serious horticulturist with shallow pockets, I recommend a greenhouse that uses soap bubble insulating technology. Insulating soap bubbles are blown into a double walled plastic film at night and are dissipated in the morning by sunshine. The water that supports the bubbles captures heat from the sun that is stored in a large tank or barrels for use when the temperature drops. Inversely, cool water is captured in the evenings and stored in another tank to be drawn upon when temperatures rise in daytime. Greenhouses are expensive to heat and cool, and using this technology will lower both costs substantially and will not contribute harmful gases to the atmosphere.

The SolaRoof concept has been around for a few decades and is used successfully in many places. SolaRoof is an open source initiative developed by Richard Nelson and others for sustainable living. Interested readers should go online and investigate the many interesting sites and comments from users of this fantastic technology. Lots of good advice is available from people glad to help; you can even visit a working SolaRoof greenhouse.

Situating the Greenhouse

No matter what the size—a small adjunct to a kitchen garden or a serious hothouse with height, doors and vents—positioning is important, as you will need maximum light in every season, especially winter. Positioning is not an easy task and may ultimately govern the size of your greenhouse. You have done all the research and know exactly what space is required for your needs—but where are you going to put it? Ideally, you want it not far from the west-facing kitchen door and close to both water and electricity. However, not living in a perfect world, your kitchen is probably on the north side of the house and your garden shaded by the tallest trees in the neighbourhood. Hunting down a place for the glasshouse to sit is never easy and requires the utmost patience. You know the size and you know the optimum direction is east west; now get some brightly coloured pegs, outline your house and try it on for a while. Walk around at all times of the day and mark the sun's progress, keeping in mind it will be lower in the sky come winter. If trees block sunshine too often, then move the pegs until you find a spot that suits both you and the house. Take your time, and eventually you will arrive at the optimum position even if it is a little off true east west. While you are in there trying on your imaginary pegged greenhouse, visualize your staging, the racks that will support your plants and your potting bench. Will there be enough room? How about the door, will it be large enough for a wheelbarrow?

Heat and Ventilation

In warmer months, controlling heat build-up in greenhouses is always a concern, depending on what plants you have installed. Orchids and tropicals need plenty of humidity, and open vents will throw that out the window and invite insect pests. That was no problem in the old days—just open the whole place up and flood it with water. The water evaporates, cools the greenhouse, maintains the humidity and makes everyone happy. Of course, with all the vents open, the greenhouse was like a smorgasbord to uninvited insects,

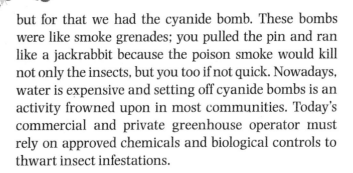

but for that we had the cyanide bomb. These bombs were like smoke grenades; you pulled the pin and ran like a jackrabbit because the poison smoke would kill not only the insects, but you too if not quick. Nowadays, water is expensive and setting off cyanide bombs is an activity frowned upon in most communities. Today's commercial and private greenhouse operator must rely on approved chemicals and biological controls to thwart insect infestations.

Canadian winters make heating glasshouses an expensive proposition unless solar energy is captured for use, but in cases of existing houses that may not be possible. Not all is lost, however, because during winter an existing greenhouse may be used as a frost-free environment to store tender ornamentals from your garden. This space can open up new vistas for gardeners and turn normally staid backyards into tropical paradises. Potted banana, orange and lemon trees, bamboo, cacti, succulents and bonsai can be enjoyed spring, summer and fall and then hauled into the frost-free space until winter passes. Only a small heater with a thermostat able to keep the temperature above 50° F is needed with proper insulation. Fresh bananas, lemons and the delightful smell of jasmine can be yours for most of the year with a frost-free—you could even buy a tiny kit for that purpose.

The company that supplies and possibly erects your greenhouse will have heating and ventilation specifications included in their sales brochures, but make sure the specifications are correct for your zone. Purchasing a heat/vent setup designed for a lower zone could mean big trouble come winter.

Shading
Ideally, you want wood slatted blinds to keep summer heat under control, but if deemed too pricey, bamboo and cheaper slatted materials are available. Barring that,

you can always do what commercial operators do and paint the outside of the greenhouse. The paint is water based, environmentally friendly and is usually gone by the end of summer. Whatever shading you deem right for your needs should be included in the initial planning, because you do not want to be surprised by an early heat wave. Grape vines planted in corners and trained to the ceiling provide wonderful shading for greenhouses and supply a yummy reward for the patience required to train the vines. Do not allow them to grow helter-skelter, but train them into an even latticework that provides maximum shade. During the couple of years required for growing and training grape vines, spray the outside of the greenhouse with shade paint. When the vines are in place, simply prune leaves to govern the amount of sunlight into the greenhouse. My grandfather employed both shade paint and grape vines to shade his orchid house, and I can still remember the huge bunches of sweet, green Niagara grapes. Walking through the orchid house in the fall was a like a hike in the Italian countryside.

Staging

Stages are the shelves your many plants will sit on. Slatted wood staging is your best bet, and you can usually order staging along with the greenhouse kit. Hinged staging is a good idea, because space is always at a premium in glasshouses. The company that supplies your kit will have staging diagrams available. Go over them carefully before ordering. Greenhouse companies will also usually offer designs for potting benches.

Greenhouse Accoutrements

Thermometer: Get a good one, and do not entertain scrimping on this instrument. You will rely upon it like an old friend. Digital readouts are fine, as long as the instrument is of good quality and the readings dependable.

Waste buckets: Get two, preferably zinc coated with wire handles. One bucket will be for organic waste destined for the compost heap, and the other for inorganic garbage.

Watering cans: Get at least two, one small 2 litre can fitted with a fine spout rose for watering seedlings, and a large 7 to 10 litre can for general use and spot watering.

Garden hose: Unless your greenhouse is expansive, buy large-diameter surgical tubing and fit the end with a good-quality nozzle capable of many spray patterns. Space is always at a premium in greenhouses, and while more expensive than normal garden hose, surgical tubing never kinks, coils easily and stores away like a dead snake.

Sprayer: You will need several sprayers—a graduated pump-style for applying insecticides or horticultural soaps, one for spot spraying water, one for backup and another for spraying shading paint.

Garden stakes and supports: Get a variety of stakes and supports ranging from small bamboo splits to wire frames and trellis for climbing vines. A good supply of labels is also a good idea, along with a waterproof marking pen.

Grow bags: No matter how full the greenhouse is, there will always be room in a corner for a grow bag or two of tomatoes, beans or cukes. Get them started early for planting outside after the danger of frost has passed, or just leave them be and pick the rewards while your neighbours are watching theirs begin to ripen.

Potting soil: A loam/compost mixture is best all around. It usually consists of 7 parts loam, 3 parts peat moss, 2 parts sharp sand with some added fertilizer and lime. Buy bags of soil as you need them so they will always remain fresh. A bag of sharp sand will come in handy, along with a bag of soil-less mixture that will usually contain peat and some fibrous material like bark or coconut husk. Use it for cutting the standard mix when starting seeds and for plants that like damp soil. Keep bags sealed tight and store in a dry place.

Knife: Get a single blade pocket variety, preferably of German make, along with a whet stone for sharpening. This knife will be your favourite greenhouse tool, and after a while, you will become as handy with it as any Naples street thug. Keep a bottle of 10% hydrogen peroxide solution to sterilize the blade after every use. Hydrogen peroxide is useful stuff, not only for sterilizing tools, but also for getting rid of some kinds of soil-borne insects, like thrips. Mix a little with water and spray the soil around plants, and in a few days, no more thrips.

Insect Pests

Biological control is the best way to control insects in greenhouses; if you have grandchildren, but little patience to entertain their curiosity, you might consider the camelback cricket. Just kidding—those things are pests and if you happen to spot one, step on it quickly before it multiplies.

What insects you will need depends on what pests need controlling, and for that you must keep your eyes peeled. The secret to controlling pests is to find 'em early. Once you have found them and know what they are, you must find a supplier of beneficial insects, a company that deliver the goods when you need them and in a number that corresponds to the size of your greenhouse. You will need the parasitic wasp for white-fly and ladybugs or midges for aphids. Beneficial insects are also available for the control of spider mites, scale and mealybugs, the latter being a main concern to tropical plant fanciers. Going online will find you a wealth of information on biological control and suppliers.

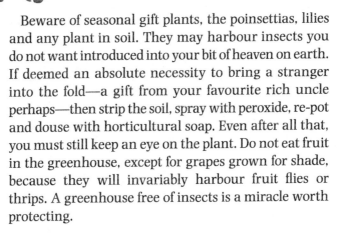

Beware of seasonal gift plants, the poinsettias, lilies and any plant in soil. They may harbour insects you do not want introduced into your bit of heaven on earth. If deemed an absolute necessity to bring a stranger into the fold—a gift from your favourite rich uncle perhaps—then strip the soil, spray with peroxide, re-pot and douse with horticultural soap. Even after all that, you must still keep an eye on the plant. Do not eat fruit in the greenhouse, except for grapes grown for shade, because they will invariably harbour fruit flies or thrips. A greenhouse free of insects is a miracle worth protecting.

Here is a list of insect pests to watch for and the biological control insects needed for eradication.

Aphids not only suck the life sap from plants, but the sticky honeydew they exude will attract ants and sooty mold. The way to get rid a greenhouse of these pests is to order a supply of the tiny wasp *Aphidius colemani*.

Mealy bugs can be a nightmare if you allow their population to get out of hand. There are two types, above ground and in ground, and both require immediate action. For the above ground, get a supply of a tiny predatory mite called *Hypoaspis*. For the root, or below ground species, drench the soil with insecticide or horticultural soap and repeat after a week.

Scale insects are almost as bad as mealy bugs, but a supply of the tiny wasp *Metaphycus* will take care of the little beasts.

Spider mites, and there are several species, but the most common in greenhouses are red spider mites. The biological control for these terrors is the predatory mite called *Amblyseius cucumeris*.

Thrips are tiny flying bugs and a headache for commercial growers, but the same bio control is used as for spider mites. *Amblyseius cucumeris* will clean them out in no time. I have used a hydrogen peroxide solution on these guys with some success. If you spot only a few, try it—spray on the leaves and around the soil.

Whitefly is a most irritating sap-sucking pest that used to drive commercial vegetable growers to drink. Now there is a little wonder wasp called *Encarsia formosa* and growers are off the juice. Marigolds also work well to ward off whitefly; a pot here and there around the greenhouse should prevent the little monsters from getting a hold.

The Future Greenhouse

Some time down the road, you may choose to live in a greenhouse; one big conservatory with a SolaRoof or similar technology to supply heat and some other new technology like cold fusion to supply electricity. Your house will filter air, capture and process rainwater for personal consumption, while a small trout or tilapia pond will supply most of the protein. Everything needed will be nearby and very alive—no more half dead salad greens and fresh fruit. Living tropical will be advantageous to both your health and pocketbook, not to mention your complexion. Europeans are already building homes that trap and store solar energy through reflective polycarbonate panels; they are greenhouses *sans* plants, but it will not be long before people catch on to the advantages of living with their own fresh food supply, especially when that habitat comes move-in ready and operational.

The technology already exists to build habitable greenhouses. At Disney's EPCOT Centre in Orlando, Florida, you can boat through a futuristic greenhouse that employs what they call an aeronic system, wherein nutrient solutions are sprayed onto the roots of plants moving on a continuous belt. It is much neater than a normal hydroponic system that requires pumping

huge volumes of nutrient solution. Visitors leave the installation with a feeling they could move right in, no problem. While normal mindset has greenhouses attached to homes, EPCOT will have you thinking homes attached to greenhouses, and why just one home. Why not multiple homes, a greenhouse co-op? Five or six homes nestled around a central greenhouse that would provide fresh, wholesome foods, filtered and humidified air, cheap, almost free heat in winter and a place to swim the daily laps. Sounds great, and hopefully property developers will hurry up the concept, as I am ready to sign on tomorrow.

A few years down the road, vertical greenhouses will begin to dot the urban landscape. People live vertically, why not food crops? Overpopulation is already straining farm production, and if the global warming trend continues to erode crop yields, vertical farms will quickly become a reality. In countries where sunshine is plentiful, but water scarce, vertical greenhouse could supply entire urban populations and relieve pressure on over-used farmlands. In developed countries, new high-rise apartments, condominiums and office buildings may have upper floors devoted to raising greenhouse crops. Buying a new condominium may include an obligation to work in the greenhouse for a few days each month in exchange for a steady supply of fresh foods. A steady supply of crops unaffected by weather and disease could stop the mad swings in the price of food in urban centres and bring stability to that marketplace.

SMART GARDENING

Gardening is rewarding work; it stimulates the body and mind and nourishes the soul. To garden is to escape life's everyday problems to a world less troubled and serene; at least, that is the goal. However, for gardeners who failed to don their thinking caps, the garden can be a place of abject disappointment. Gardeners need to plan their every move before the season begins so it can be a time of heaven on earth. Not usually a problem, because most gardeners love plot 'n' plan and pour over gardening books and magazines during the long winter.

To keep vegetable plants safe from insects without chemical insecticides, consider pairing them up with a Judas plant. Aphid infestations are a plague to vegetable gardeners and may affect a variety of crops, especially tomatoes. Aphids love tomato plants, but they absolutely adore nasturtiums. Planting nasturtiums near tomatoes will attract aphids and make them easy to deal with by removing and discarding the nasturtium plants.

When weeding the periphery of a vegetable garden, the wise gardener might consider leaving a few milkweed plants, as they attract not only butterflies, but cutworms too. Both mustard and columbine make excellent bug traps and are easy to remove along with the bug infestation.

Herbs, the Garden Insect Repellents
What is a garden without herbs—and many species serve a dual purpose. Basil and sage are both kitchen

standbys and each produces a chemical that repels flying insects. Both are a boon to the smart gardener and planted near tomatoes will both improve the flavour of the fruit and protect it from insects.

Oregano will keep bugs off cabbages and cucumbers, while chives will protect both tomatoes and carrots. Catnip will keep ants away, while sage will discourage slugs.

Companion Planting

Some plants have friends to protect them from insects. Borage interspersed among your tomato plants will discourage tomato worm. Catnip will keep beetles off your eggplants, while regular mint will defend cabbages from aphids and beetles. Nasturtium, marigold, pennyroyal, petunia and hyssop make wonderful borders for vegetable gardens and do a great job defending against insects.

FACTS

Researchers at Iowa State University have discovered that nepetalactone, the essential oil in common catnip, is 10 times more effective at repelling mosquitoes than commercial repellents containing the chemical DEET.

Mosquitoes dislike the oil in citronella plants because it irritates their feet.

There are around 2700 species of mosquitoes and they are found on every continent except Antarctica.

Mosquitoes are voracious pests to Canadian gardeners. Your best bet to control them is to patrol your yard for standing water. Make sure eavestroughs are clean and not pooling water. Check under shrubs for discarded bottles or cans. Make sure garbage containers are not collecting water and your wheelbarrow is turned upside down. Follow water after a heavy rainfall and make sure it is not pooling in ditches. Ornamental ponds with no fish should be filtered or treated with larvicide and birdbaths hosed out daily. Be relentless; find that standing water and your mosquito problem should disappear. If not, then get your neighbours to check for standing water—the beasts are coming from there.

Lemon grass works well to discourage mosquitoes. It will not survive a Canadian winter, so treat it as an annual or over-winter in a garage or frost-free greenhouse. Lemon grass also makes an excellent personal mosquito repellent: simply crush the stem's tender bottom part and apply it to skin or make an infusion in alcohol.

Most commercial bird feed contains some weed seed. Locate birdfeeders as far from your gardens as possible, preferably over a hard surface to prevent germination of seeds.

Birdfeeders frequented by non-native house sparrows may inflate local sparrow populations and deprive songbirds of nesting sites.

Doubling Crop Production

It can sometimes be a gamble, depending on the weather, but smart gardeners will want to plant an additional crop late in the season. Your raised beds have yielded a fantastic seasonal crop of vegetables and you could not be happier, but the sun still shines and the beds look ready for more. Do it! Get out the garden fork, give the soil a turn and plant late summer lettuce or any of the Brassica family crops such as cabbage, Brussels sprouts, cauliflower or broccoli. Cut tops off plastic milk containers to use as emergency cloches for young plants in case of inclement weather.

With a bit of luck, your beds will yield up a bounty of goodness even as the snow flies. You cannot do it every year, because the beds need some winter fallow time, but every three years should be fine as long as you remember to manure well in the fall. Who does not love a steaming bowl of cauliflower soup when those winter winds begin to howl? By doubling up, you can have fresh, tasty greens on the table and be something of a hero to your family and friends. Lovin' from the oven takes on a completely new meaning when food comes fresh from your garden.

Patch Planting

Long raised beds may be interspersed with smaller, square beds for the exclusive use of one vegetable or a variety of herbs. Herbs love being "off in a corner" and will dazzle and dance you into thinking "I should have done this before." A raised bed herb patch will keep herbs like mint from escaping and will turn the daily collection into a joyous experience. If aromatic herbs are your thing, separate lavender, mint and basil off from culinary herbs by a parterre, which is a simple hedge of dwarf boxwood that if clipped hard and square imparts a neat, formal look to your raised bed.

Asparagus is another crop that benefits from patch growing, and it is sad that many gardeners do not even consider asparagus when planting beds. There is almost nothing so delicious as a plate of fat, juicy asparagus spears. Asparagus is similar to corn in that it will lose sugar and begin to turn starchy the moment of picking. To have either growing just steps away from the boiling pot is heaven—your family or dinner guests will think they have never tasted anything so tender and delicious.

Asparagus needs room, so your patch should be a large bed in full sun, preferably against a wall or fence to protect it from wind. Take time to prepare the bed for planting—you will be entering into a long-term agreement with a crop that produces for over 20 years. Fork in plenty of well-rotted manure and remove all weeds. In summer, a few days before planting, scatter some slow-release fertilizer granules over the bed and turn the soil again. You will be planting crowns, not seeds, onto a mound. Make a trench 30 centimetres deep and 20 centimetres wide and fill with loose soil to make a 10 centimetre-high mounds. Carefully place the asparagus crowns onto the mounds, spreading the roots out on either side. Set the crowns 30 centimetres apart and cover with 5 centimetres of sifted soil. Trenches should be 30 centimetres apart.

As the crowns begin to grow, cover them with additional sifted soil. Do not allow the crowns to dry out. Before winter, cut down the foliage to 5 centimetres above ground. That is all you need do, and except for resisting the temptation to cut the spears for two years and weeding, you are in for a glorious relationship.

In two years, when the spears are 12 centimetres long, use a serrated knife to cut them 7 centimetres below the soil. Place them into boiling water immediately. You may cut spears until mid-June, when you must stop and let the crowns gather energy for winter.

Tomato Patching

Tomatoes attract insects, especially when planted in rows. To mix things up for the insects, try planting tomatoes in patches, a few plants in one raised bed and a few plants in another. The tomatoes will benefit and you can avoid spraying with insecticides.

Potato Patching

Potatoes do nicely in raised beds, but to get the most bang for the buck, you will need the soil in the raised bed to be much deeper than normal. You need to construct a spud box and you will be glad for it, mostly because it makes for an easy harvest of your bounteous crop. A spud box is simply a 122 square centimetre, or 4' × 4', raised bed with 2" × 6" planks attached to four pre-drilled 5' corner posts: a crate. But the magic lies in how you plant your potatoes—you screw on half the side boards, fill the spud box with the finest, fluffiest soil you can make or find, and plant your potatoes. Then, as the spuds begin to grow, you add another board and more soil until you reach the top. This slow addition of soil forces the potato plants' roots deeper, and that will result in a cornucopia of tubers at harvest time. To harvest your crop, you simply unscrew the boards, rake out the soil and remove your potatoes. Dry the component parts of your spud box and store in a handy place ready for spring planting.

Tools

The right tool for the right job is a truism applicable to almost any manual endeavour, especially construction and gardening. You would not think of building without power tools, and while gardening is basic toil in the soil, it pays to maintain the same power tool mindset. Garden tools should do maximum work with minimum effort, and if yours are raising too much sweat on the brow, hop over to your local garden centre and test drive some new tools. If you are new to gardening or beginning fresh, all's the better, because you will not be saddled with hand-me-down implements and garden junk. Here is a list of basic tools needed by every gardener and my personal slant on each.

Wheelbarrow: Aside from shovels, a wheelbarrow is your most important garden implement and the one most likely to turn time in paradise into drudgery. Too small, too big, too shallow, too heavy and a tendency to tip at the wrong times are all common problems with the ubiquitous metal garden donkey. Gardeners become attached to these horrors and provide them with names, like Ol' Rusty or Squeaky, but if you have one of these abominations, get rid of it, and I do not mean recycling it into a planter. What you need is a heavy-duty, plastic wheelbarrow with deep bin and a ball or wide wheel. For all the years I owned and operated a garden centre in Toronto, this type of wheelbarrow was indispensable. We sold wheelbarrows, all kinds and models, but our favourite was the plastic donkey with the ball wheel. They hold a lot, are easy to turn, never rust, dent or have flat tires and they stand up to unbelievable abuse no matter what size the garden.

Shovels are the most important tools in your armoury. You will need three—one flat head shovel and two spades, a normal and a narrow blade nurseryman's spade. Do not scrimp—buy the best available and make sure they are stainless steel and sharp. If they have dull blades, talk nice to the store manager and perhaps he or she will sharpen them for you.

Pruning shears: Once again, do not scrimp. The cheaper shears will entice, but the more expensive quality shears will last a lifetime and become old friends. A good pair of scissors is another must-have tool.

Rakes: You will need three—a hard tine, a broom and a shrub rake. Buy only metal with wood handles and eschew plastic or bamboo. Do not consider for one moment buying a leaf blower even if your neighbours already have one. If there is ever to be a list of inventions the world could do without, leaf blowers will be at the top, next to frozen French fries.

Garden hose: Buy the best all-rubber hose with heavy brass fittings that money can buy. Anything else will waste your time and drive you to drink.

Trowels are indispensable for planting, scooping soil into pots, and removing weeds. Buy two, with stainless steel blades and wood handles.

Hedge clippers: Great for trimming hedges, but you will find a hundred other uses. At the golf course, I use hedge clippers as much as pruning shears, especially for cutting back flowering perennials for a second, end-of-summer go around.

Edger: Flowerbeds need a nice clean edge and with this tool, you get that. Once again, get the best and have it sharpened. Stainless steel, wood handle and make sure there is a lip for pressing down with your foot.

Hoes: Buy the one with three tines; it is a more efficient tool than the standard hoe. If your beds are extensive, you might consider adding one with four prongs along with a hula hoe. The hula has a squashed circular-shaped working end that slips under the soil to nip off the roots of small annoying weeds. It works great in loose, well-worked soil. Another great hoe, especially good for getting in close to mature plants, is a winged hoe, or weeder. This tool has a triangular head with sharp edges and is handy for fast weeding.

Garden forks are great for turning manure and other organics into soil, but there is a better alternative, the power tool.

Electric or gas-powered soil tiller: Get one of these time savers and do your back a big favour. No matter what size the garden, there is a power tiller to suit your requirements. There are small electric tillers of different sizes and shapes to suit raised bed gardens, and there are the mule like, gas-powered tillers for more expansive gardens. I know, I know, you are the hands-on type of gardener who revels in feeling the earth give and fold to the tines of the ol' garden fork. Trust me, once you try an electric tiller you will kick yourself for being a Johnny come lately while you spend all that saved time on more rewarding tasks, like planning the tool shed.

Garden shed: It should be not too big, not too small, but proportional to the size of garden and gardener. If the former is sizeable and the latter not a bit handy at construction, hire a contractor, buy a kit or install a ready-made from a local lumber company. Cedar is best, but if adding to property value is not a concern, any wood or metal will do nicely. Wooden structures, including cedar, should be kept from touching the ground to prevent rot and insect infestation, while metal sheds should be immediately planted around with vines to be more in tune with nature. The shed should have at least one window and be sturdy enough to support tools hanging from walls and a few shelves for all the small stuff. Shelves are often integral to garden shed construction, which is a good thing since you can never have too many shelves. While planning the shed, keep a future greenhouse in mind and place it at the shady end of a sunny east-west track. A well-designed cedar garden shed makes an ideal entrance and work area for a greenhouse. Just an idea, one that might catch your fancy at some later date, so better position the shed on an east-west axis.

FACTS

Municipal water that contains fluoride will cause brown tips to form on most tropical plant leaves. To fix this problem, use watering cans for tropicals and allow the water to age a few hours before using.

Well and pond water may contain high levels of minerals injurious to plants. Check these sources of water for pH and mineral content before using as a greenhouse water supply, and install a filter to trap algae.

Around 5680 litres of fresh water are required to manufacture 1 barrel of beer.

About 25,000 litres of water is required to grow a day's food supply for a family of four people.

ENGINEERING A GARDEN

Gardens are your basic refugee camp in the nature-vs-nature battlefield. Flowers or vegetables, the little guys you plant will be happy to be there and will look to you for all the necessities of life: water, food, protection and love. Love is a requirement of all successful gardeners and the guiding factor in determining the size and what goes into a garden. Large houses invoke visions of shady bowers, garden follies and vast swaths of flowering annuals. Nice, but a Victorian pipe dream unless you are prepared to hire some extra love in the form of a professional gardener. If you are building new or moving into a large house needing landscape design, hire a professional, as he or she will know how much love you have to spread among your charges. If time or water is a factor, he or she will probably recommend a perennial garden and the plants to set. However, if you have the time, water and enough love, nothing beats the annual flowerbeds; they sooth the soul with their happiness and make you glad to be alive.

Flowerbeds usually border fencing or sections of the house not shaded by trees, and they may extend for entire lengths or be broken into smaller sections by circumstance. With older properties, circumstance usually means trees, as it was the custom in times gone by to plant them as property markers. Congenial neighbours did not build fences in those days; they grew hedges between the property marker trees. Nowadays, people are so security conscious they have both hedging and a fence. Whatever you have, that is where you

construct your flowerbeds and you need to plan them well to avoid disappointments down the road.

If you live in an older house, you will need to put your garden plan on paper and plot available sunshine within your property boundaries. Plotting sunshine is simply observing the path of shadows that may darken your flowerbed, whether from trees or the house itself. Take observations of available sunshine at different times of the day, two in the morning and four in the afternoon. Available sunshine will dictate what annual bedding plants and bulbs will go where, as full sun is required for the popular bulb flowers. Tulips, daffodils, iris and gladiolus are bulb sets that require full sun and look their best in mass planting—a sometimes difficult undertaking for today's homeowner, especially in tree-shaded cities. Full sun is gold to gardeners, so mark yours well and keep in mind that newly planted shrubs and trees are tomorrow's shadows.

Once you have your areas of full sun mapped out, mark down the partly sunny areas and shade. What you have on paper are the garden parameters, what you can grow and where to put them. Simply go online or visit your local plant nursery and secure a list of full sun, part sun and shade-loving flowering plants and bulbs.

The smart gardener will construct a vegetable garden with raised beds; it looks neater, is easier on the back, warms faster and provides plants with better drainage than old ground level beds. You can buy raised bed kits, or if you are handy with tools, you can build your own. Dozens of online sites exist to provide instructions. The beds can be any length, while width is usually determined by the reach of the gardener—you must be able to reach the middle of the bed comfortably, so reach × 2 is the norm. The beds can be any height, but higher means more soil to fill, and depending on ease of access may require dozens of trips with a wheelbarrow.

If installing raised beds in a property being land-scaped, do the beds first, because the nurseryman's dump truck can unload directly into the beds. New properties should have soil under beds checked for contaminants, and if any are found and remediation is thought unnecessary or impractical, raise the height of the beds slightly and lay down heavy plastic sheeting under every one before assembly.

The Hydroponic Kitchen Garden

Small countertop hydroponic units are popular and work well, but are limited to producing a round of burger topping and a small salad for the family barbecue. In planning a larger, more serious hydroponic kitchen garden, consider available space, ventilation, humidity, what greens to plant, the expected harvest and costs. Large hydroponic installations are a serious undertaking, with nutrient tanks, pumps, tubes and timers, and are best left to professionals. Let your fingers do the walking and phone a professional for a construction quote. If you find that a trifle daunting and want to test the water first, buy a large floor-model kit—they are easy to assemble and with a few crops under your belt, you will know to "yeah" or "nay" a permanent installation.

Facts

The artificial light best suited for hydroponics is called High Intensity Discharge, or HID lights, and they are designed to illuminate with the correct spectrum of light waves and are ideal for growing plants indoors.

The average yield of tomatoes grown in soil is around 10 tons per acre, while an acre of hydroponic-grown tomatoes will yield around 200 tons.

Butterfly Gardens

Butterflies are the angels in your bit of heaven. Flitting through sunbeams, sitting motionless on a blossom, wings gently moving—and then off they go leaving you wishing they would stay a while. They probably would stay, if only the garden had what they needed, nectar and a host plant to lay eggs.

To attract butterflies into a garden requires both, and the Government of Canada has a comprehensive list of butterflies found in Canada and their requirements posted online. I am in awe of Monarch butterflies—whenever I see one I feel like throwing my hat into the air and cheering. Seeing them in fall is like watching Charles Lindberg heading for the Atlantic and on to Paris, but without the coffee and sandwiches.

Monarchs can fly 50 kilometres per hour at heights of over 1 kilometre. They are the only butterflies capable of transoceanic flight and are frequently spotted in Europe, New Zealand and Australia. Canadian Monarchs migrate like birds and over-winter in Mexico, and while they start back in the spring, only the females make it as far as the first milkweed patch. There she deposits her eggs and dies. However, directions to home are genetically passed to her offspring and when out of pupae stage, they continue the journey. To the Monarch, there is no birth or death, only the journey to home. A bit reminiscent of the Garden of Eden story, with mankind getting the boot and beginning the long journey back into the Creator's good graces.

If you want to keep these tiny angels in your garden, you must have milkweed hosts, as Monarchs can sip nectar from many different flowering plants, but will only lay eggs in the milkweed.

Facts

There are 292 species of butterflies in Canada; 176 are native to British Columbia.

Next to bees, butterflies are the main pollinators of plants.

The larvae of some butterflies establish symbiotic relationships with ants. The larvae excrete honeydew, a sugary food, while the ants provide protection from predators. Honeydew-excreting larvae can communicate with ants by producing various sounds.

Canada's largest butterfly, the Giant Swallowtail, can have a wingspan of almost 13 centimetres.

The Fragrance Garden

Corners of expansive gardens or small fenced backyards can both become olfactory pleasure gardens to rival those of any sultan or maharaja. In early times, people looked upon bathing as a dangerous undertaking: respiratory diseases were rampant, and bathing got the blame, a stigma that lasted right into the 20th century. Historically, people stunk, but in European cities they were used to it, as evil smells permeated their every waking moment—and what is a little body odour compared to the smell of open sewers and rotting garbage?

During the 17th and 18th centuries, wealthy people resided outside of the cities, and while they did not have the daily odours to contend with, they still stunk of body odour and horses. The French hid personal odours by an

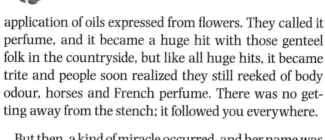

application of oils expressed from flowers. They called it perfume, and it became a huge hit with those genteel folk in the countryside, but like all huge hits, it became trite and people soon realized they still reeked of body odour, horses and French perfume. There was no getting away from the stench; it followed you everywhere.

But then, a kind of miracle occurred, and her name was Josephine, wife of Napoleon Bonaparte. During her husband's Egyptian campaign in 1798, botanical studies were undertaken and plant seeds gathered, some from a plant that intrigued Josephine. That plant was *Reseda odorata*, an herb known to the Romans and used as a sleeping potion. Perhaps a need for sleep caused Josephine to plant the shrubby herb in her gardens at Malmaison. Whatever the reason, what popped out of the ground smelled divine and earned from her the name *mignonettes*, meaning "little darlings." What Josephine grew in her gardens, others had to grow too, and the honey/raspberry scent of the mignonettes spread through southern France like wildfire all the way to England.

Every home, even in the cities, featured a pot or two of mignonettes. In the country, they went into the truck gardens of manor houses. Manor house gardeners, overwhelmed by guests wanting an olfactory experience, soon had the mignonettes in their own space, the pleasure garden. Pleasure gardens became so popular that gardeners sought out and added other fragrant plants: roses, sweet peas, machet and a host of others. Pleasure gardens became integral to genteel country living until the advent of central heat and plumbing, then people began to bathe and the pleasure gardens became distilled into bars of soap.

Fragrant soaps were late arrivals to Canada. By the dawn of the 20th century, there were around 200 automobiles in Canada and about that many bathtubs. However, the spectre of the pleasure garden had followed immigrants to the New World, and almost every home garden featured a small area set aside for fragrant plants including Josephine's little darlings, the mignonettes.

Today pleasure gardens are once again increasing in popularity as gardeners discover the healing, calming affect of fragrant plants. Some gardeners even take the concept one step further by adding another dimension to their pleasure garden: a theme, with monochromatic fragrant flowers like white gardenia, stephanotis and roses, or even a moon garden, with fragrant flowers that open only at night.

SOME FRAGRANT PLANTS

The Annuals

Flowering Tobacco	Nasturtium
Heliotrope	Scented Geraniums
Lemon Basil	Sweet Alyssum
Mignonette	Sweet Pea

The Perennials

Artemisia	Lemon Verbena
Bee Balm	Lily (a few)
Chrysanthemum (a few)	Lily of the Valley
Daylily (a few)	Peony
Evening Primrose	Poet's Narcissus
Hyacinth	Red Valerian
Hyssop	Sweet Rocket
Iris (a few)	Sweet Sultan
Lavender	Sweet Woodruff
Lemon Mint	

Woody Plants and Vines

Black Locust	Citrus
Carolina Allspice	Clethra
Chilean Glory Vine	Honeysuckle
Chinese Jujube	*Hoya carnosa*

Lilac	Roses
Linden	Snowball Viburnum
Mock Orange	

Exotics

Cestrum nocturnum	Jasmine
Cruel Plant	Queen of the Night
Gardenia	Stephanotis

Fragrance gardens can serve a dual purpose, enjoyed when the flowers are in bloom and saved for a scent of summer to dispel mid-winter blues. Making potpourris is a cinch. The general rule for mixing is ¾ dried aromatic flower blossoms to ¼ dried leaves. For each quart of dried mixed material, add 1 cup of fixative, like camphor oil or dried orrisroot and 1 Tbsp of your favourite spice, like cinnamon or cloves. Do not dry your flower blooms in the sun—they will bleach and lose scent. Laying them out on a table and drying gently with an electric fan is a proven best way to dry them.

During my years of operating a greenhouse and garden centre I must have made a ton of potpourri from the hundreds of exotics that went through our hands—lemon blossoms, jasmine, gardenia. I mixed them all and would sometimes come up with potpourris that smelled like heaven. Lots of fun, but try not to get carried away chopping blossoms, because it will turn your garden into a war zone. Gardeners who get into drying aromatic blossoms for potpourri will usually have a corner of the flower garden that is expendable, a place behind the bushes where nobody ever looks.

The Palette Garden

To many gardeners, planning is half the fun. They spend winters are spent curled up beside a roaring fire perusing all manner of seed and garden catalogues deciding what annuals go where and how many. For years, you have been doing the spring shop at the local garden centre and have returned with the same standard mix of annuals and sweet alyssum for borders.

Only this year, you have decided on something entirely different—this spring you are going to have some real fun. You are going to paint with flowers. You have the garden down on paper, the perennials are marked in, and the blank sections are your canvas. You will be the artist gardener and your colour palette is that pile of catalogues. Like the artist Claude Monet, you will lay on the colours with a heavy brush stroke. No mixing, not this spring, this will be the year of bold, concentrated colour, big splashes of yellow, red, blue and white, a feast for the eyes and a whole lot of fun for you.

Palette gardens are common to golf courses and large institutions. At the golf club, we are partial to perennials of solid colour—black-eyed Susans, daisies, coneflowers and alliums. Happy time plants—and you can get the same effect in a smaller garden with annuals: red and blue cornflowers are so dazzling they are almost hypnotic.

The Water Garden

Nothing soothes the spirit like the music of falling water, and nowadays gardeners can have their spirits soothed inexpensively by using kits. Kits are available to power waterfalls without ponds, with ponds and even from one container to another, Japanese style. However, if you can afford the luxury, the waterfall and pond is magic, and if the pond is large enough to support water lilies and fish, it is over-the-top sublime. A water feature in any flower garden, be it pond or fountain, changes the ambience from one of mild interest to an almost hypnotic rapture.

CONCLUSIONS

And the Lord God planted a garden eastward in Eden;
and there he put the man whom he had formed.

—Genesis 2:8.

Many people doubt the existence of the Garden of Eden and consider the story from Genesis to be just that, a story. The doubters are wrong, of course, and for substantial argument they simply have to look into a mirror, as we are the substance. We are the Adam and Eve, and the Genesis story is but a condensed version of the transition of mankind from a hunter/gatherer existence to an agrarian lifestyle.

According to Dr. Juris Zarins, of Southwest Missouri State University in Springfield—a man who spent years researching the subject—the Genesis tale began 30,000 years before the birth of Christ, with mankind evolving from slow-witted Neanderthal to a modern, quick-to-learn version. In those early times, the great ice age gripped most of Eurasia and sea levels were some 120 metres below today's level, leaving the area of the Persian Gulf high and dry but irrigated by four great rivers, the still-existing Tigris and Euphrates and the long-gone Gihon and Pison rivers. This most fertile area was a garden paradise to those newly transitioned people forced to constantly move about in a desperate quest for food.

However, according to Dr. Zarins, this area was not the Garden of Eden, because that occurred many years later as a result of climate change. Around 15,000 BC, the rain stopped falling, and the aridity caused the retreat of Paleolithic populations to an area historians call the "Fertile Crescent," the eastern Mediterranean to the Indus River valley and south to the Nile.

Years later, around 6000 BC, in what climatologists call the Neolithic Wet Phase, the rains returned to the Persian Gulf area and it once again became a verdant green paradise. The people returned, most to forage food, but some arrivals had learned to make the food come to them, to plant and harvest. The Genesis story now comes into focus, because transition from forager to agronomist was a miracle of the first water; the Creator had given mankind a garden called Eden.

Well and good, but how about that part in Genesis where mankind bites the apple and gets the boot from the garden? Well, according to Dr. Zarins, when foragers migrated back to the Persian Gulf area and encountered people already raising crops and livestock, they resented it.

In Dr. Zarin's own words,

> The whole Garden of Eden story, however, when finally written, could be seen to represent the point of view of the hunter-gatherers. It was the result of tension between the two groups, the collision of two ways of life. Adam and Eve were heirs to natural bounty. They had everything they needed. But they sinned and were expelled. How did they sin? By challenging God's very omnipotence. In so doing, they represented the agriculturists, the upstarts who insisted on taking matters into their own hands, relying upon their knowledge and their own skills rather than on His bounty.

There were no journalists around to record the tension, no historians. However, the event did not go unnoticed. It became a part of collective memory and finally, it was

written down, highly condensed, in Genesis. It was very brief, but brevity doesn't mean lack of significance.

Weird how it all fits when looked at from a story perspective, with farmers in white hats being run off the range by rustlers in black hats. But even off and running, the white hats hung onto their miracle, and the garden that was Eden became like the parable of the loaves and fishes. The knowledge kept dividing, and nowadays just about every person on the planet knows how to make the food come to him or her.

Fact is, the miracle of the Garden of Eden is so ingrained in human psyche that it has become almost a genetic trait. We are made in the Creator's image with dominion over a garden paradise. It is surely a class, Paradise 101, and we are flunking big time. How will we explain the damage? What will we say when the Creator asks about the whales? What excuse can we offer for turning those majestic creatures into lamp oil and sushi snacks?

To walk among the redwood and sequoia trees is to feel their holiness, and we turn them into patio furniture. We have fouled the Earth and our fresh water with chemicals unknown even to the Creator. We have changed the chemistry of the seas, made the air unfit to breathe, and every day 500 new chemicals are added to the witch's brew. There are no excuses, and the only reason we are not already pillars of salt is the Creator's infinite patience. We have to fix it—no question, because the Genesis story has no ending and will continue until one is attained, either good or bad. For all the Neanderthal mess we have made, our blue planet is still the Garden of Eden, but without remediate action we are out the door like rats from a sinking ship.

Fixing the mess will not be easy. It will require a global consensus to begin repairing the damage, but it will only take three steps.

Step 1—Rein in unfettered population growth, something the Chinese have already attempted with their one child per family law. India has also made some inroads in controlling population, but by 2050, India will be the most populous country on the planet with 1.63 billion people, a shameful 50% increase over 2008. India is a disaster waiting to happen, and many African countries are in the same leaky boat—two successive crop failures and there will be no more boat. By 2050, more than a third of the world's people will live in Asian countries, and if their present pollution trends continue, the entire world will suffer their prodigious excesses. Asian politicians not afraid of a hot potato issue must realize the prognosis and take some action before disaster strikes.

Step 2—Return the world to sustainability—easier, but it will require global consensus to work. We cannot continue using up global resources like no tomorrow, because tomorrow is already here and we have nowhere to go when it runs out. We are born to die on this planet and 100 *Star Trek* reruns ain't going to change that fact one iota, so we had better hunker down and start rationing what we have or that will soon be nothing.

Step 3—Stop the garbage—the easiest of all. Before World War II, water came from the tap, milk came in returnable bottles, vegetable peelings went into the composter, nothing came double wrapped and a kid with a wagon collected newspapers. In a little more than half a century, the world has almost buried itself in plastic and aluminum containers because throwaway is easier than returns and industry only cares about the bottom line.

In Canada, butter used to come wrapped in parchment paper, but then along came a French-owned multinational dairy concern with a cultured butter franchise. Good stuff, and a big Quebec dairy co-op

bought into the deal, but the French dairy conglomerate required their product be wrapped in aluminum foil, which added about 5% to the retail price. The Quebec dairy cooperative whined to Ottawa, the Canadian aluminum companies spread around some goodwill, and our federal government passed a law requiring butter to be wrapped in aluminum foil, no matter that it cost more and consumers were happy with the parchment. You could cut butter in parchment with the back of a knife and simply pull it from the wrapping. Parchment was a convenient and cheap packaging material that must have cost the aluminum companies and that Quebec dairy cooperative a fortune to bury. Weird how nobody objected to paying more and having to pick off bits of aluminium foil from the butter, but that was progress, only nowadays progress is killing the planet and not to do something is insanity.

Three steps, how hard can it be: slow the breeding, stop cutting the forests, and nix the garbage. Three moves and the sun will shine on the Garden of Eden. It seems so simple, but when politicians are involved webs must be weaved and nothing is simple. Meanwhile, while the politicians weave, gardeners have their little bits of Eden that insure them something good and fresh on the table and flowers to brighten the night.

The best place to seek God is in a garden. You can dig for him there.

—George Bernard Shaw